Valley Interfaith
and School Reform

Joe R. and Teresa Lozano Long Series
in Latin American and Latino Art and Culture

Valley Interfaith and School Reform

Organizing for Power in South Texas

DENNIS SHIRLEY

University of Texas Press, Austin

First edition, 2002

Requests for permission to reproduce material from this work should be sent to Permissions, University of Texas Press, Box 7819, Austin, TX 78713-7819.

⊚ The paper used in this book meets the minimum requirements of ANSI/NISO Z39.48-1992 (R1997) (Permanence of Paper).

LIBRARY OF CONGRESS CATALOGING-IN-PUBLICATION DATA
Shirley, Dennis, 1955–
Valley Interfaith and school reform : organizing for power in South Texas / Dennis Shirley.— 1st ed.
    p.   cm. — (Joe R. and Teresa Lozano Long series in Latin American and Latino art and culture)
Includes bibliographical references and index.
ISBN 0-292-77764-7 (alk. paper) — ISBN 0-292-77765-5 (pbk. : alk. paper)
    1. Education—Rio Grande Valley.   2. Educational change— Rio Grande Valley.   3. Community and school—Rio Grande Valley.   4. Valley Interfaith (Organization)   5. Rio Grande Valley—Social conditions.   I. Title.   II. Series.
LA371.R56   S55   2002
370'.9764'4—dc21   2001034789

With all of my love to
Skye and Gabriel

CONTENTS

The greater border region

South Texas. *Source:* David Montejano, *Anglos and Mexicans in the Making of Texas, 1836–1986* (Austin: University of Texas Press, 1987).

ACKNOWLEDGMENTS

This book could never have been written without the extraordinary contributions of many different people. I will always be indebted to Connie Maheshwari, Salvador Flores, Yolanda Castillo, Estela Sosa-Garza, Sister Pearl Ceasar, Sister Judy Donovan, Father Bart Flaat, Sister Maria Sánchez, Rosi Ruiz, René Ramirez, and Carmen Anaya for hosting me during my many visits to their schools and communities in the Rio Grande Valley of Texas. Ernie Cortés, Oralia Garza-Cortés, Tim McCluskey, Sister Consuelo Tovar, Sister Christine Stephens, Elizabeth Valdez, Carissa Baldwin, and Jim Drake provided me with many valuable insights into conditions in the Valley and the origins and development of political struggles along the U.S.-Mexican border.

Many scholars read through early drafts of this book and provided helpful comments that compelled me to sharpen my analysis and to dig more deeply into the data. I am grateful to Mary Brabeck, Brinton Lykes, Angela Valenzuela, Emilio Zamora, Courtney Cazden, Richard Murnane, Chandler Davidson, Walt Haney, and Guadalupe San Miguel Jr. for their careful readings and incisive criticisms. Zen Camacho, your constant enthusiasm and support for this work have meant so much to me. Maria Brisk, Frank Guajardo, and Lawrence Hernandez—thank you for our stimulating conversations about linguistic and cultural diversity.

Several students at Boston College provided me with critical assistance in completing this project. Aaron Ramirez, Steven Blaum, Brianne Chai-Onn, Tito Cruz, Cathy Horn, Tina Zhuo, and Kuldhir Bhati—thank you for your fun-loving sense of humor, patience, and friendships as we moved this manuscript through the final months of preparation.

The research for this book was supported by the Annenberg Rural Challenge, Research Incentive Grants from Boston College, and the

President's Travel Fund from Rice University. I would like to thank Vito Perrone for inviting me to work with the Research and Evaluation Team of the Annenberg Rural Challenge and for his helpful comments on early drafts of this manuscript. I am also grateful to Howard Gardner, who hosted me as a Visiting Scholar at Harvard Project Zero during a sabbatical year from Rice, and provided me with a stimulating environment for transcribing my field notes and beginning this book.

Finally, I would like to thank my family for your love, which sustained me throughout the writing of this book. Skye and Gabriel, you can't imagine how much your companionship and those wonderful hugs when I came home in the evening have meant to me. Shelley, thanks once again for standing by me and tolerating my frequent absences and endless obsessions about this project.

COMMUNITY ORGANIZING IN THE RIO GRANDE VALLEY

The frontier between the United States and Mexico—which until the Second World War was the site of relatively modest population migration—has in the postwar era turned into one of the most dynamic and heavily traversed national boundaries in the world. The explosive growth of Mexican-origin populations in the major U.S. metropolitan regions has wrought dramatic changes upon North America's demographic, cultural, political, and economic landscapes. Concurrent with these broad changes, the educational system in the United States has sought to respond to Mexican immigration with a broad range of initiatives, of which bilingual education is perhaps the most salient, but in actuality represents merely one component of a broader movement for greater multicultural awareness and linguistic sensitivity in our nation's schools.[1]

The changes wrought by Mexican immigration have had an impact on the economy, politics, and culture of the United States in countless ways. Yet while much ink has been spilled concerning the challenges confronting the United States, U.S. citizens of Mexican origin, and Mexican immigrants in the current context, we are only just beginning to articulate a broader vision of educational theory and practice that can integrate these demographic transformations into a democratic synthesis that will enhance a rich civic life for immigrants and citizens alike. This topic is of increasing urgency because of both the growth of the Mexican and Mexican American populations in the United States and the imperative that future citizens have at least the foundations of an education that will enable them to participate in the nation's civic and economic life. Such analytic work is crucial if we are to sustain and extend our nation's democratic and republican legacy, both for Americans who have resided here for many generations and for the immigrants who seek opportunities in the U.S. economy and polity that they have been denied in their homelands.[2]

The current study is an effort to address this lacuna in scholarship by describing the efforts of a community-based organization in the South Texas borderlands to improve the living conditions of low-income citizens and immigrants and the public schools their children attend. This work is significant because the worlds of community organizing and school reform have been distinct from one another until relatively recently. Community organizers addressed glaring injustices facing poor and working-class communities that pertained to health care, job opportunities, and crime, but refrained from tackling issues relevant to school reform. Educational reformers, on the other hand, focused on pedagogical, curricular, and assessment issues in schools without addressing the problems of unemployment, crime, and inadequate health care that have a disproportionate impact on low-income communities.

The self-imposed boundaries thus established by community organizers and educators made sense to a degree, given the inability of any single group to address the staggering number of problems that confront poor and working-class communities. However, they impeded the exploration of common ground and the kind of intellectual exchange that can occur when individuals from different cultural and class backgrounds commit themselves to sustained learning from one another. Only recently have systematic efforts begun, predominantly in metropolitan areas of the Southwest, to cross boundaries and to examine both how community organizing can catalyze the work of school reform and how transformations in a school can give a politically disconnected community a locus for civic engagement. The initial results of these efforts have been intriguing and call for further study in other settings that reflect the diversity of the American civic and cultural landscape.[3]

A second indication of the significance of this work has to do with larger issues confronting public education in the United States in the current political and economic conjuncture. For a variety of reasons, Americans' faith in their public schools is at a historic low, and surveys indicate that a majority of Americans would now prefer to send their children to private schools if expense were not an issue. At the same time, recent economic trends have exerted a downward pressure on the wages of poor and working-class Americans and have caused the United States—once the proud bastion of a strong middle class—to become the world's most economically stratified developed country. When combined with other data tracking a decline of civic engagement and secondary associations over the last thirty years in the United States, the net effect is a troubling portrait of a society characterized by a decline in citizenship and the "brasilianification" of the economy. While these trends have been problematic for many adults, they have been catastrophic for children growing up in conditions of poverty. In this context it is imperative to learn about countervailing efforts to mend the fabric of everyday life and promote the civic engagement that is the sine qua non of free and pluralistic societies.[4]

A third aspect of this work has to do with the changing nature of classroom instruction in the United States. Partly as a result of the poor showing of American children in international comparisons but also driven by the political opportunities afforded by a troubled educational system, American reformers have developed a massive battery of high-stakes standardized tests over the last fifteen years. It has become increasingly apparent to observers that those tests now determine a significant portion of the de facto instructional, curricular, and assessment practices in public schools in the United States. Preliminary research indicates that test-driven reforms dominate the practices of schools serving low-income and minority children more than those serving white, middle-class children. Teachers in South Texas are under extraordinary pressures to demonstrate that their students have mastered academic subject areas such as reading, writing, and mathematics. At the same time, the teachers are aware that their children come from communities that lack the economic infrastructure that most Americans take for granted, and that problems with crime, substance abuse, and lack of access to health care afflict their communities at disproportionately high rates. How the schools and communities grapple with these challenges, and aspire to academic excellence at the same time that they recognize and seek to overcome debilitating conditions of poverty, defines the central terms of debate for educators and community organizers in the accounts that follow.[5]

By attending to the issues entailed in high-stakes standardized testing in public schools and integrating data on test scores into the narrative and analysis, this account does not in any manner seek to endorse uncritically the use of such tests as the Texas Assessment of Academic Skills (TAAS). Numerous studies have documented that standardized testing has often been used in a manner injurious to the educational interests of some students, particularly minorities, but also girls and women. Even if a test has high degrees of reliability and validity for individuals, it can still be used by others—whether they be teachers, testing experts, business leaders, or politicians—in ways detrimental to the test-takers. Walter Haney has argued that what is key in interpreting test results is not their predictive power but their "educational validity"—that is, the extent that they help individuals to continue to learn. "And from a more positive perspective," Haney wrote, "what is needed is to use test results not so much to make decisions about individual students, as to examine critically how our schools are serving their interests." It is in this sense that the present study incorporates test score results into both description and analysis.[6]

Thus, the following account seeks to describe innovative work fusing community organizing and school reform in a regional setting characterized by high rates of immigration of families from Mexico. To accomplish these purposes I shall first describe the origins of the community organization known as Valley Interfaith that has struggled for more than fifteen years to improve housing conditions, health care, employment opportunities, and schools in the Rio Grande Valley in Texas. I shall then present case studies of three schools that have collaborated with Valley Interfaith and struggled to increase parental engagement, address pressing community needs, and achieve high levels of academic success. Finally, I note points of comparison and contrast between the schools, and indicate those areas that appear most fruitful, as well as those that seem problematic, for future explorations in the intersection of school reform and community organizing.

SOCIAL CAPITAL THEORY

The theoretical framework guiding these investigations is informed by recent work in political science, economics, and sociology that indicates research into the *social capital* of a community can go far in explaining both its strengths and its problems. In contrast to *financial capital*, which designates the value of money, or *human capital*, which refers to an individual's intellectual and physical capabilities, social capital comprises the values embedded in social relationships. A grandmother or an aunt who provides child care in the afternoon for children while their parents work reflects one *informal* kind of social capital, while social capital can also be *formalized* through institutional arrangements such as a Girl Scouts chapter, a PTA, or a congregation. In addition, social scientists also distinguish between *bonding* social capital—which occurs among individuals in an institutional setting such as a church or trade union—and *bridging* social capital, which refers to strong lateral ties between individuals across organizational boundaries. In terms of schools, I will refer to bonding social capital as that which strengthens social ties among teachers or between teachers and students, whereas bridging social capital will designate ties that can be created between teachers, clergy, and community activists.[7]

Social capital theory has recently been brought to bear on a wide range of topics confronting American society, from low voting patterns to school failure to crime. At first advanced tentatively by economist Glenn Loury, the idea was then developed with more rigor by sociologist James Coleman, who applied it to explain what he perceived as the superior achievement of Catholic schools in educating low-income urban youths. It was not until political scientist Robert Putnam published his now famous essay "Bowling Alone," however, that social capital theory gained widespread popularity as an explanation for fin-de-siècle malaise in the American body politic.[8]

"Bowling Alone" identified a pervasive disengagement of Americans from civic institutions and social life. According to Putnam, Americans over the last quarter century withdrew from trade unions, PTAs, and face-to-face voluntary associations on a historically unprecedented scale. Putnam suggested that this disengagement manifested itself through a drop both in voting and in participation in mediating institutions such as churches and civic clubs, as well as through a decline in social trust. In its most dramatic expression, social decapitalization appeared to reflect the problems of a society that had lost its moral bearings and cultivated individualism and materialism at the expense of sociability and an ethic of mutual responsibility.

Putnam's "Bowling Alone" was easily the most influential monograph of its type to appear in the 1990s, and it spawned a veritable industry of scholarly research on social capital even before an expanded version of the argument appeared in book form in the summer of 2000. It is intriguing to note that even when critics attacked Putnam's findings they generally did not question the utility of social capital theory as a framework for evaluating social problems. Andrew Greeley, for example, took Putnam to task for failing to acknowledge the concentration of social capital in religious institutions in the United States, but explicitly sought to refine social capital theory in the process. Similarly, Alejandro Portes criticized Putnam's use of the concept for its "logical circularity," believing that Putnam construed the concept in such a way that it was both a cause and an effect of virtually every social problem in contemporary American society. Like Greeley, Portes sought to circumscribe the boundaries of social capital more clearly to ensure that the notion would maintain its conceptual rigor.[9]

The work at hand seeks to maintain this spirit of creative reconceptualization and development of social capital theory, in this case at the nexus of education and community engagement. Recognizing that social capital theory is in the infancy of its development—just as human capital theory was a generation ago—we must anticipate that only continued theoretical and empirical work will clarify whether social capital will develop into a truly robust concept that can clarify hitherto obscure facets of social life. In the current study, I endeavor to use social capital theory to explore contemporary efforts in the overlapping terrain of school reform and community organizing in three South Texas schools and communities. I also seek to criticize and refine social capital theory by distinguishing between different kinds of school and community ties and underlining their varying ramifications. For example, there is a world of difference between a *parental involvement* strategy in a school that uses parents for cafeteria duty or photocopying and a *parental engagement* approach that develops parents' leadership capacities to attack social injustices in a school or community. Likewise, the potential for social capitalization is far greater in a school in which a principal works actively with local religious institutions and community organizations to enhance culturally congruent pedagogy and curricula than in a school where a disconnected administration adopts a laissez-faire attitude toward parents and their community. Precisely because "parental involvement" or "community outreach" are such widely accepted slogans in contemporary American education, theoretical rigor in disaggregating robust social ties from their more superficial counterparts is of some urgency if we are to develop public schools as centers of civic engagement rather than islands of bureaucracy that are devoted more to district and state mandates than to the communities they serve.[10]

Throughout the narratives that follow, we shall explore whether the concept of social capital can bear the amount of theoretical weight attached to it in recent contributions in the social sciences. If parents become more engaged in their children's school and in community development, does that engagement necessarily translate into increased academic achievement for children? James Coleman suggested that social capital explained the superior outcomes from Catholic school education over public schools in inner-city communities, but subsequent commentators have noted that Coleman's analysis was fundamentally flawed, for two reasons. First, Coleman's study focused on academic achievement at the high school level, but the youths in his study typically did not come from a parish in close proximity to a school, but rather from a scattered metropolitan area. Second, the parents were more or less involved in a fiducial relationship with the school; they trusted and supported the school's authority, but were not otherwise particularly engaged with it.[11]

In spite of this incisive criticism of the fundamental premises of Coleman's work, the notion that social capitalization could cause high levels of academic achievement has continued to provoke interest among sociologists of education. One gets the impression from much of the social capital literature that social capitalization is a cure-all not only for student learning, but for almost every other problem that afflicts American society. In the case studies that follow, a more complex portrait will emerge—one in which social capitalization has many benefits but in which a pattern of causation in terms of raising academic achievement is ambiguous. These findings will then lead into a more nuanced inquiry, in which social capitalization has an intrinsic worth in terms of its contributions to human relationships and community development, but is not viewed as a panacea either for the multitude of problems that confront underresourced communities in general or for issues relating to student academic achievement in particular.

In addition, we shall also explore what might be referred to as the "hidden costs of social capitalization." Extensive research indicates that school reform efforts typically assign classroom teachers hosts of new responsibilities without any corresponding relief from the already demanding tasks of planning instruction, teaching classes, and fulfilling administrative requirements. This phenomenon of "intensification" can cause teachers to lose a focus on student learning, expend valuable time on issues peripheral to their vocation, and in extreme cases leave their profession. If social capital theory is to make a lasting contribution to school reform, its adherents must recognize the problems inherent in intensification and develop strategies to assure that instruction by classroom teachers is not compromised, but enhanced.[12]

Although social capital theory is in need of further elaboration, even in its current incarnation it offers a crucial and often missing analytic tool for those who are concerned with the political and economic problems that characterize contemporary American civil society. Rather than the reigning methodological "individualism" that studies institutions and social phenomena in relative isolation from one another, social capital theory is interested in the nexus between institutions, cultures, and group norms. This last point is particularly important, because by recognizing that values infuse and shape social relationships, social capital theory challenges both functionalist and structuralist schools of social analysis and restores the centrality of norms to social inquiry. Finally, social capital theory, with its explicit interest in secondary associations and civil society, provides a heuristic device that can diagnose problematic areas in which social networks have weakened and, at least potentially, lead to strategies that will strengthen those networks that exist in the interstices beyond the reach of both the state and capitalism. It can thus generate new forms of knowledge in the key intermediate zone of "civil society" that entails families, religious institutions, and neighborhood associations and that exists between the bureaucracies of the welfare state and the vagaries of the marketplace.[13]

THE RIO GRANDE VALLEY

The region called the Rio Grande Valley in South Texas belongs to a swath of land known as the "Trans-Nueces" that was wrested from Mexico by the United States after the Mexican War under the terms of the Treaty of Guadalupe Hidalgo in 1848. In subsequent decades Anglo-Americans settled the region and gained an upper hand in both the economics and politics of the Valley—as it is called by locals and Texans in general—freely exercising extralegal forms of political intimidation and establishing a dual labor market that discriminated against indigenous Mexican and Mexican American campesinos and workers. Tragically, the leadership of the Catholic Church in the region played an important role in reinforcing rather than challenging the anti-Mexican racism of the Anglo-American elite.[14]

The native Mexican population did not respond passively to the incursions of the Anglo-American settlers; rather, it mixed forms of accommodation to North American culture with both spontaneous and organized forms of political resistance. These included outright rebellion, with a call to restore land to Mexicans deprived of their land after the annexation (the Cortina War); individual acts of self-assertion against the rule of South Texas lawmen (Gregorio Cortez); and a series of raids against Texas Ranger patrols and United States Army detachments as part of a determined campaign to drive Anglo-Americans out of the American West (*los sediciosos*).[15]

In the late 1800s and early 1900s, with the growth of railroad lines west of the port city of Brownsville, Anglo-American economic penetration of the Valley increased; and the region was settled by a new wave of land speculators, sugarcane planters, citrus farmers, and merchants, all of whom sought to capitalize on plentiful land, cheap labor, and a rapidly expanding consumer market. In this same time period a host of new communities were established whose names bear the marks of their Scottish immigrant and Anglo-American founders, such as McAllen, Edinburg, Harlingen, and Pharr. In spite of some positive indicators, however, economic growth lagged behind the rest of the country. Although the Valley increased its agricultural output dramatically throughout the following decades, by the early 1970s McAllen, the largest city in Hidalgo County, was the poorest metropolitan area in the entire United States.[16]

More recently, the Valley has undergone some of the strongest population growth in the United States. Propelled by the establishment of a free trade zone just north of the Rio Grande, maquiladoras on the Mexican side, and the anticipation by international investors that the region is likely to experience economic growth, the Valley's trajectory offers a point of contrast to other rural areas in the United States that have suffered economic decline and massive out-migration in the last quarter century. In addition, the commercial success of the Chicana singer Selena and the *boleros, corridos,* and *norteños* that she popularized have created greater curiosity and interest in the region's culture from Americans of all walks of life.[17]

While positive developments have occurred in the Valley, however, a host of indicators reflect a deeply troubled region. More than a third of the predominantly Hispanic population in the Valley is poor, and unemployment rates have fluctuated between more than double to almost quadruple Texas state averages in the last twenty-five years. Education is a key problem for Valley residents: more than half of the adult population over eighteen years old has not completed high school, and many citizens and immigrants lack the linguistic and technical skills to participate in an economy in which knowledge plays an increasingly decisive role in determining the value of wage labor. Environmental analysts concur that the Rio Grande, the primary waterway that sustains the Valley, is by far the most polluted river in North America. As if economic, environmental, and educational woes were not enough, Valley residents suffer a variety of health problems—such as gastroenteritis, tuberculosis, hepatitis, diabetes, and various skin diseases—at rates three to six times the national average. Finally, the passage of the

North American Free Trade Agreement (NAFTA) in 1994 has proven to be a massive disappointment for the residents of the Valley, who have watched jobs continue to head south of the border, where wages are far lower. Most of the major economic decisions that impact the region continue to be made in distant places such as Dallas, Houston, and Mexico City.[18]

The problems encountered by Valley residents are therefore severe when measured against the standard of living that most citizens of the United States and other industrialized nations take for granted. Some of the problems—low rates of formal education, a population disproportionately impacted by a restructuring economy, and restricted access to health care—mirror problems experienced by Latinos on a national scale, while others reflect the increasing stratification of wealth and the growth of child poverty that are national and multiethnic in scope. While these problems clearly call out for multifaceted and bold experiments in social policy—perhaps modeled on strategies developed by other industrialized nations—it is also becoming increasingly clear that education, perhaps more than any other single factor, is absolutely essential to acquire the income needed to sustain a family with a middle-class standard of living in the United States for the foreseeable future. It is therefore imperative to document experiments in school reform and renewal that can enable traditionally disenfranchised populations to enjoy the fruits of an education that will enhance their economic opportunities and enable them to experience both the pleasures and challenges of engagement in American civil society.[19]

It is in this context that the work at hand is important. In what follows, I first describe the origins of Valley Interfaith, a grassroots community organization in the Rio Grande Valley. Describing both the political and social context of the Valley and the singular nature of Valley Interfaith's broad-based organizing effort is central if one seeks to comprehend the nature of its impact in the region. The narrative then turns to three case studies of schools in Hidalgo County that have sought to increase both academic achievement and political engagement on behalf of children and families through collaboration with parents, congregations, and Valley Interfaith. I begin with Palmer Elementary School, located in Pharr, and trace the origin of its collaboration with Valley Interfaith back to issues pertaining to the impoverished communities it served in the 1980s; I will then examine how teachers, administrators, and parents at Palmer used those issues to develop social capital for purposes of school reform. The narrative then turns to Alamo Middle

School, which was transformed in its first ten years from a crisis-ridden school characterized by repeated outbursts of youth violence and administrative paralysis to a learning community with a team structure that allows for personalization of instruction and deepened community ties. Finally, I end with Sam Houston Elementary School in McAllen, and investigate the manner in which this school's struggles for high academic achievement have been nurtured through its collaborative relationship with the parish of Saint Joseph's the Worker Catholic Church.

The methodology employed in conducting this research is qualitative and consists of a mixture of snowball sampling, focus group interviews, ethnographic classroom observation, and the selective incorporation of quantitative data such as test score results, student attendance records, and the number of students in bilingual education classes. Test score results for the schools, along with comparable data for their districts and economically disadvantaged students in Texas, are presented in tabular form in the appendix. To enhance social trust and to test the veracity of my research I regularly sent drafts of my writing to community organizers, principals, teachers, and clergy and nuns involved in school reform. I found that the calculated risk of sharing research—while being perfectly clear that the research must contain a critical component—not only increased the richness of my documentation but also deepened my relationships with my informants, who were eager to gain another perspective on their work. Given the reality that social science research in the United States is inextricably enmeshed in issues of ethnicity, language, gender, and class, a deliberately dialogic methodology seemed a fruitful strategy for building relationships between the researcher and community members and mutually enhancing the reflectivity of all involved.[20]

While conducting previous research on the collaboration of urban schools with community-based organizations in Texas for the book *Community Organizing for Urban School Reform,* I documented the work of metropolitan organizations affiliated with the Texas Industrial Areas Foundation in a network of schools called "Alliance Schools." However, I chose not to address community-organizing work that had occurred in the Rio Grande Valley. Cautioned by the writings of border scholars Américo Paredes and José Limón, I believed that folding the Valley into a collection of case studies on urban schools would more likely obscure than illuminate the cultural and political dynamics of the region. Rather, I intended to develop a separate study of community organizing and school reform in the Valley that would recognize the cultural complexity and uniqueness of the Lower Border while simultaneously attending to the specific etiology of school reform work in that context. The present work is the result of those considerations.[21]

The research was conducted through a series of site visits to Palmer Elementary, Sam Houston Elementary, and Alamo Middle School from the spring of 1997 to the fall of 1999. In addition, I also interviewed activists in other community organizations working with farmworkers and undocumented immigrants; made home visits with parent liaisons and principals; attended Valley Interfaith activities such as press conferences, "accountability sessions," and the fifteenth-anniversary celebration in Edinburg in March 1998; interviewed political leaders such as McAllen mayor Othal Brand, Texas Governor Ann Richards, and Lieutenant Governor Bill Hobby; attended Mass at Saint Joseph's the Worker Catholic Church in McAllen; enjoyed forays across the border to restaurants in Reynosa and Las Flores for cabrito with my always gracious and generous hosts; and (last but not least) survived Hurricane Bret in August 1999. As with my previous research, I decided that my investigation was likely to be most fruitful if I focused on schools where the community-organizing work was most developed rather than on those that were just beginning a partnership with Valley Interfaith.

In conducting this research I have endeavored to triangulate my findings to check for the use of hyperbole or other forms of distortion in my informants' comments. As with any account of this nature, it is susceptible to confirmation bias, in which the researcher's sympathies with informants impede the development of an impartial and balanced perspective. To correct against this possibility, I sought out teachers, parents, students, politicians, and clergy who had made critical comments about Valley Interfaith and the schools under investigation, and have woven their perspectives into the ensuing narratives and analysis. The resulting portrait endeavors to combine a mixture of hope at small victories garnered in classrooms and communities as well as realism about the daunting challenges facing children, parents, educators, and congregations in the South Texas borderlands.

Valley Interfaith
and School Reform

CHAPTER ONE

FOUNDING VALLEY INTERFAITH

The Origins of a Grassroots Organization

The Rio Grande Valley of Texas has an unusually rich and complex history as a region of the United States. Wrested from Mexico as part of the Treaty of Guadalupe Hidalgo, it has ever since been marked by alternating periods of contestation and accommodation with the dominant culture in the United States. For the first two-thirds of the twentieth century Mexican immigrants and Mexican Americans in the Valley had to adjust to a dual labor market that had many similarities to the Jim Crow South. Mexican immigrants and Mexican Americans attended segregated schools and were denied entrance to public facilities such as restaurants, hotels, swimming pools, and movie theaters. Their children suffered humiliating punishments when they spoke Spanish—even outside of formal instruction—while attending public schools.[1]

The cultural and political oppression experienced by Mexican Americans and Mexican immigrants was not suffered in silence. Voluntary associations provided a cultural framework in which Hispanics could celebrate a common identity, and over the decades intermittent outbursts of trade union organizing, inspired by Mexicanist traditions of syndicalism, characterized social and political life in the Rio Grande Valley. Larger national groups such as the League of United Latin American Citizens (LULAC) and the GI Forum made important gains in the years since World War II, and together with African American and Native American civic organizations slowly pushed the nation toward greater equality for minorities. In spite of their gains, however, it was not until the 1960s that a real sea change in the direction of greater civic equality was truly achieved by Mexican Americans in the Rio Grande Valley.[2]

The initial transformation of South Texas politics in the 1960s began with John F. Kennedy's campaign for the presidency. United States citizens of Mexican descent had traditionally been discounted by politicians because of low voter turnout, but this pattern changed through the power of the "Viva Kennedy" campaign, which rallied many citizens in South Texas to support the Democratic candidate and was central to the Kennedy victory in Texas. Building on that momentum, Hispanics founded a political coalition encompassing hitherto separate groups such as the GI Forum and LULAC into a powerful new entity called the Political Association of Spanish-Speaking Organizations (PASSO). Then, in 1963, PASSO, working together with the Teamsters Union, organized the first electoral defeat of an Anglo-American elite in a South Texas city. The location was Crystal City, and the victory has since been characterized by historian David Montejano as the first major symbolic "overthrow of Jim Crow" in South Texas.[3]

PASSO's achievement, however, came with a price, as moderates defected from the organization while militants, savoring their first electoral triumph, sought further opportunities to advance the political condition of Americans of Mexican descent. The next opportunity came in the form of a wildcat melon strike, which was hastily organized by the United Farm Workers (UFW) at the massive La Casita farms in Starr County in 1966. The strike developed considerable momentum in its first weeks, and at one point UFW organizer Gil Padilla pulled off an organizing coup when he enlisted the support of the Confederación de Trabajadores Mexicanos, one of Mexico's strongest unions, on behalf of the strike. Padilla's accomplishment was significant because one of the greatest challenges for union organizing in the borderlands traditionally had been the easy availability of strikebreakers from the Mexican side of the Rio Grande. For a variety of reasons, however, the strike collapsed, and the UFW subsequently decided to concentrate its efforts in California.[4]

The defeat of the UFW in Starr County hardly marked the end of political organizing in South Texas; on the contrary, it sparked a reconceptualization of organizing strategy. Frustrated by the outcome of the strike, youthful Chicano activists including José Angel Gutierrez and Willie Velasquez founded the Mexican American Youth Organization (MAYO), which subsequently developed chapters in the Rio Grande Valley in Weslaco, San Juan, Pharr, Edcouch-Elsa, Harlingen, Alamo, and Brownsville. School walkouts by students in Pharr–San Juan–Alamo and Edcouch-Elsa in 1969 served as crystallizing events that promoted demonstrations and Chicano activism throughout the region. In 1970 Gutierrez played the leadership role in organizing La Raza Unida, the first Mexican American political party, and won electoral victories in Crystal City, Cotulla, and Carrizo Springs during the same year. In February 1971 Alfonso Laredo Flores, a twenty-year-old construction worker, was killed during a rally against police brutality in Pharr, and his death served as another catalyzing point for MAYO and the UFW in the Valley. Finally, the Catholic Church, led by a series of activist archbishops in San Antonio, began playing a major leadership role on behalf of migrant farmworkers, supporting the UFW's national grape and lettuce boycotts, and concentrating resources from the Campaign for Human Development in parishes along the Lower Border.[5]

For many, the changes in the political climate in South Texas during the late 1960s and early 1970s were long-overdue victories that secured a more just and inclusive social order. Yet it is important to note that the victories came at considerable cost. While many lay Catholics were thrilled by the social activism of Archbishop Robert Lucey in San Antonio, Lucey failed to combine his desire for improved conditions for Mexican American campesinos and workers with greater democratization within the Church itself. As a result, a coalition of priests who had once been his strongest allies turned against him and forced him from office in 1968. As for La Raza Unida, José Angel Gutierrez's inflammatory rhetoric frightened many Anglos in South Texas, and there was such an exodus of Anglos out of Crystal City after the elections of 1970 that the local Rotary Club folded and the Lions' Club lost half of its members. The Mexican American Youth Organization, which had done so much to promote Chicano activism in South Texas, was folded into La Raza Unida Party in 1972, and La Raza Unida itself collapsed shortly thereafter, undermined by internal polarization, the indictment of officials for the misuse of public funds, and the arrest of key leaders on marijuana-smuggling charges. Finally, more traditional forms of union organizing fell flat, and the Amalgamated Clothing and Textile Workers' Union (ACTWU), which tried to organize a Haggar's textile plant in the Valley, found that workers' fears of strikebreakers from across the border prevented any chance of a successful strike to raise wages and improve conditions.[6]

By the early 1980s, the Valley once again had two major political powers, the Democrats and the Republicans, and while broader national trends toward greater equity for minorities and the growth of a Mexican American middle class had produced important changes for some, the vast majority of Valley residents still struggled with a precarious economic existence and little political power. The leadership of the Catholic Church viewed the situation with grave concern. "It was a desperate time for us," John Joseph Fitzpatrick, the bishop of the diocese in Brownsville recalled, "and I knew I had to do something." Bishop Fitzpatrick was particularly troubled by the persistence of problems in the "colonias," unincorporated neighborhoods developed by realtors that often lacked basic infrastructure such as water lines, drainage, and paved roads. Although such communities were rare in the rest of the United States, roughly 34,000 people—10 percent of the total Valley population—lived in colonias in Willacy, Cameron, and Hidalgo Counties at that time.[7]

As Bishop Fitzpatrick began exploring possibilities for attacking some of the most glaring political and economic injustices in the Valley, he consulted with Patrick Flores, the archbishop of San Antonio, and himself a former migrant worker. Flores informed Fitzpatrick about a new kind of citizen's organization called Communities Organized for Public Services (COPS) in San Antonio, which had developed civic power and had forced that city's political elite to allocate desperately needed funds to improve drainage, road repair, and parks on the city's predominantly Hispanic West Side in the 1970s. Fitzpatrick learned that COPS had an institutional base in San Antonio's parishes, which paid dues to support organizers and infrastructure. He further learned that COPS was one of a number of community organizations around the country that was affiliated with the Industrial Areas Foundation (IAF), which had been founded by Saul Alinsky in Chicago in 1940. After meeting with other Texas bishops and local clergy, nuns, and laity to discuss the matter, Fitzpatrick decided to take a risk and invite IAF organizer Ernie Cortés to develop a similar kind of organization in the Valley.[8]

Ernie Cortés had a long history in community-organizing work before he tried to develop an IAF group in the Valley. He had organized the statewide boycott of La Casita melons for the UFW during the Starr County strike. Cortés experienced the strike's failure both as a political disaster and as an important object lesson in the unintended consequences that can result from hastily organized labor militancy. He subsequently spearheaded the efforts of the Mexican American Unity Council in San Antonio to create more minority-owned businesses in the city, and he trained with IAF groups in Milwaukee, Wisconsin, and East Chicago, Indiana, in the early 1970s. Through his training he learned the nuts-and-bolts of community organizing as developed by veteran IAF organizers such as Saul Alinsky, Nicholas von Hoffman, Ed Chambers, and Fred Ross. He then returned to Texas, where he laid the groundwork for the creation of COPS in San Antonio, and a sister organization, called The Metropolitan Organization (TMO), in Houston.

It was thus a propitious turn of events when Cortés received an invitation to return to the Valley sixteen years later to begin a new community organization that would be affiliated with the IAF. Cortés rented an apartment in McAllen and began a series of conversations with clergy, nuns, and local leaders in the Valley. These conversations then expanded into dozens of small group meetings in parishes and homes throughout the Valley in 1981 and 1982. Cortés approached the meetings not with concrete expectations of what should happen but rather with a deeply rooted concern about the grievances that citizens encountered as part of their everyday lives. In Catholic churches, schools, community centers, and homes in small towns such as Mercedes, Pharr, and Weslaco, as well as in cities such as McAllen, Harlingen, and Brownsville, Cortés sought to understand the nature of local problems confronting Valley residents. "We talked to everyone," Cortés recalled, "not just farmworkers and assembly-line workers, but also teachers, superintendents, real estate people, and small business people." In addition to the face-to-face conversations that facilitated interpersonal trust, Cortés also convened four three-day workshops at churches throughout the Valley to explore the economic and political problems of the area and test individuals' readiness to take some leadership in a new IAF organization.[9]

At this juncture it is important to observe the contrast between Cortés' organizing strategy and previous political mobilizations that had transpired in the Valley. Cortés was not attempting to organize solely farmworkers, as the UFW had done; nor was his effort concentrated solely on ethnicity, as was the case with La Raza Unida; nor did he focus on a generational cohort, as was the case with the Mexican American Youth Organization. Instead, he sought to develop a broad-based organization with stakeholders from across class, ethnic, linguistic, and generational lines. The hope was that by not only bringing together people with a shared group identity but also combining those groups with others who had traditionally been disconnected from one another that a new and more powerful kind of community organization could be developed. In other words, Cortés was pushing beyond the strengthening of *bonding* forms of social capital to develop more fruitful kinds of *bridging* social capital that would reconfigure the social networks of community leaders in the Valley.

Many issues emerged from the meetings Cortés convened at churches and community centers. At the top of the list were community concerns about colonias, schools' lack of adequate funding, toxic waste disposal in Port Isabel, and a long-standing struggle to obtain workmen's compensation benefits for migrant laborers. Gradually, Cortés began identifying problems, winning the trust of Valley residents, and locating talented individuals who could provide the energy to help a new community organization take off and seriously address the pervasive problems of the Valley.

In reviewing the formation of a group such as Valley Interfaith, it is important to understand the internal operations of IAF organizations. *Organizers*, such as Ernie Cortés, were paid salaries out of dues raised by a sponsoring committee, which in this case was led by religious institutions in the Valley. All of the priests, nuns, and laity who sought to support Valley Interfaith—such as those who served and worshiped at Saint Joseph's the Worker in McAllen, Saint Margaret's in Pharr, and Immaculate Conception in Brownsville—discussed the work of the new organization and held elections with their parish councils to vote democratically on whether they should support it.

Leaders, on the other hand, were local community residents who received guidance and training from organizers and in fact waged the political fights themselves. One of the major principles of IAF organizing is the "iron rule" that one should never do for others what they can do for themselves. In the community organizing work carried out in the Valley, Cortés questioned, agitated, and coached Valley residents, but the developing political work—which would soon expand to include voter registration, the upgrading of Texas' indigent health care, and the equalization of school funding—was carried out by the indigenous population itself.

In addition, IAF organizers and leaders work with a specific community organizing strategy that organizers impart to leaders through a kind of "assisted performance" that is richly contextualized in nature. For example, organizers teach leaders to do disciplined interviews with community residents—called "one-on-one's" in IAF jargon—in which leaders learn to ascertain individuals' passions and commitments in brief, task-oriented exchanges. "House meetings"—another cornerstone of IAF organizing—consist of small convocations of individuals in homes in which leaders learn to address the most grievous injustices in their communities and translate inchoate sources of anger into concrete issues that can be addressed in the political arena. "Research actions"—yet another step in the organizing process—consist of the acquisition of new knowledge, whether through meetings with school board members or city councilors or through a guided study of the budget of a school or a public works program. In each of these instances, the IAF works as a deliberately educational organization that enables individuals to understand, work with, and challenge power holders among business and political groups in their cities.[10]

An important part of this work for organizers in South Texas involved understanding the complex nature of the population in the Valley. A large population of migrant workers of Mexican origin was based in the Valley, but was often out of state, scattered from California to New York, gathering crops from late spring to early autumn. In addition, a number of those migrant farmworkers were *indocumentados*—Mexicans without official approval to reside in the United States—who lived in townships along the border and were afraid of being deported back to Mexico and especially cautious about any kind of political involvement or controversy. To complicate matters further, a flood of refugees from state-sponsored terrorism in Central America entered South Texas in the early 1980s, and Bishop Fitzpatrick opened a shelter for them called Casa Romero in Brownsville. The Casa fed (on his estimation) roughly two and a half million meals to over 150,000 refugees from El Salvador, Nicaragua, and Guatemala. Finally, a large and settled population of Mexican American citizens of the United States, along with a small percentage of Anglos, also made up Valley demographics, with only a tiny sprinkling of African Americans and Asian immigrants scattered throughout the Valley.

Ernie Cortés played the key role in organizing hundreds of meetings in homes, churches, and community centers in the Valley in 1981 and 1982, and he found that Bishop Fitzpatrick's ministry was of vital importance in helping the organizing drive. "We had a lot of trouble starting EPISO [the El Paso Interreligious Sponsoring Organization] at the same time that Valley Interfaith began," Cortés recalled. "People would come to our meetings and find out afterwards that their tires were slashed. The local press really went after us, calling us outside agitators and digging up stuff on Alinsky and the politics of confrontation to scare people. One of the big reasons that it didn't occur in the Valley was because of the extraordinary leadership of Bishop Fitzpatrick."[11]

Cortés' organizing work paid off with the creation of the new

IAF group in the summer of 1983. Cortés himself wished to name the new group "VIVA," which would stand for "Valley Interfaith—Values, Action," but the congregations and their leadership preferred the shorter "Valley Interfaith." Financially, Valley Interfaith was supported by roughly half the Catholic parishes in Hidalgo, Willacy, and Cameron Counties as well as Protestants from a half dozen denominations, including Methodists, Presbyterians, and members of the United Church of Christ. Additional financial support was drawn from the ACTWU and the Campaign for Human Development, the social-action branch of the Catholic Church.

If the previous experiences of COPS in San Antonio and The Metropolitan Organization in Houston had been followed, Valley Interfaith would have next focused on an effort to redirect local resources to address the most pressing needs of the working poor. This precedent was not followed, however, because "research actions" that focused on the economic resources of the Valley indicated that there were few local resources to target. Although there were a few large farms and industries, those were the exception rather than the rule; the Valley on the whole was poor. Hidalgo County had the dubious distinction of having the lowest average income per wage earner in the United States ($6,011); Cameron County's average was only slightly better ($6,654). A third of Valley residents received food stamps. Community organizing in the semirural impoverished borderlands would require a different kind of political strategy from that developed in Texas' metropolitan areas. Unlike its organizing efforts in San Antonio and Houston—where the effort focused on redirecting city revenues into poor communities—the low level of financial capital in the Valley would call for a novel strategy appropriate to the unusual conditions in South Texas.[12]

In addition to the role of poverty, a second, perhaps more perplexing problem concerning political disorganization also characterized the Lower Rio Grande. "The Valley has been kind of balkanized historically," Ernie Cortés commented. "The communities see themselves in competition with one another. They've never had a regional, common thread." One early Valley Interfaith leader, Javier Parra, lamented the provincialism that he felt characterized the Valley: "I always saw myself as coming from Brownsville, and I never really thought about whether I had anything in common with people that were living in Edinburg, McAllen, or Donna." That kind of parochialism resulted in a frequent wasting of precious resources; thus, although they are all within an hour's drive of each other, McAllen, Harlingen, and Brownsville all have their own metropolitan airports. While the Valley did have a rich political history and a wide number of civic associations grounded in Mexicanist cultural traditions, it tended to be richer in conflict than in consensus.[13]

In this context, Valley Interfaith developed a strategy not of organizing *against* the state but *toward* the state. The political tactic developed by Valley Interfaith involved a complex process of local self-education about the availability of state-controlled resources and the necessity of targeting them through a carefully nurtured development of political strength. "Valley Interfaith got right away into the state arena," organizer Tim McCluskey recalled, "because there wasn't any tax base in the Valley for schools and there were feces in people's water supply. We saw problems like these and we knew that we had to go after them right away." After a series of workshops to educate citizens and immigrants about the availability of resources at the state level, Valley Interfaith began a voter registration drive. Its efforts complemented the ongoing efforts of Willie Velasquez, the executive director of the Southwest Voter Registration Project, to register tens of thousands of citizens in the Lower Border who had not exercised their right to vote.[14]

Part of Valley Interfaith's early work involved developing relationships with the state's political leaders. Fortunately for Ernie Cortés, Ann Richards was the state treasurer of Texas at that time, and she had long admired his work with the disenfranchised in the Lone Star State. "I had first met Ernie during the La Casita boycott when I was a housewife in Dallas in the 1960s," she recalled, "and we would go to grocery stores together to try to get the melons out of there." Like Cortés, she was deeply concerned about the poverty of the Valley. "I was very conscious of South Texas," she recalled, "because the tax dollars always seemed to go to the big cities—San Antonio, Houston, and Dallas—and that was true whether you were talking about highway dollars, schools, or anything else." Along with Governor Mark White and Lieutenant Governor Bill Hobby, Richards was given tours of colonias by Valley Interfaith and asked to support funding proposals to improve conditions in the rural settlements. Much to the surprise and delight of colonias residents, she was able to deliver on a series of multimillion dollar grants to upgrade the colonias throughout the 1980s.[15]

Another major area of political struggle that initiated the work of Valley Interfaith was work on improving school funding. For years Texas' notoriously stratified system of school financing had provoked lawsuits and legislative debates, driven initially by a case in Edgewood

ISD in San Antonio, but expanded upon over many years of litigation. At issue was a school-funding system that was so decentralized that the state's most affluent districts were allocating more than twenty times the per pupil spending than the state's poorest districts. Reflecting long-standing racial and ethnic inequalities, the most affluent districts were predominantly White while the poorest were predominantly Black and Hispanic, so the *Edgewood* case was keenly watched by low-income minority communities desperate for greater access to public funds.

To respond to the inequities and to promote a dramatic improvement of public schooling in Texas in the early 1980s, Governor Mark White, a Democrat, sought to develop comprehensive and bipartisan legislation in the Texas House and Senate to improve the public schools. Governor White circumvented teachers' unions—even though they had supported him in the election—and created a Select Committee on Public Education (SCOPE), headed by computer magnate H. Ross Perot, to recommend a radical overhaul of the state's educational system. In the ensuing months SCOPE members set to work educating themselves about the politics of education in Texas, identifying the key problems they wanted to attack, and meeting with teachers and parents to inform themselves about the broad range of public opinion.[16]

The schools in the Rio Grande Valley had some of the state's highest concentrations of low-income students—easily outdistancing that of metropolitan areas such as Houston or Dallas—and Valley Interfaith organizers and leaders moved quickly to educate themselves about the issues at stake with SCOPE's work. Although IAF organizations traditionally were reticent to take on educational issues—aside from an experimental schools project in Chicago that failed in the 1960s—the unfairness of the funding system was so egregious, and parental concern in the Valley was so great that Valley Interfaith leaders and organizers felt compelled to become engaged in the school reform debate. Thus, the organization began a series of research actions into Texas' byzantine system of school funding. This effort gradually evolved into a series of workshops in parishes, schools, and homes throughout the Valley that focused on the state's maldistribution of school funds and potential strategies that could bring more revenues to the Valley's schools. Valley Interfaith established ties to Ross Perot, who was impressed with the research local leaders had done on complicated financial issues related to school funding; it pushed educational and human resource development more broadly to the top of the political agenda in a region that had often been dominated by the economic concerns of a small number of powerful farmers; it demonstrated that a congregationally based community organization could become a powerful advocate for the reform of public schools.[17]

This burgeoning political clout was channeled into forms that had concrete political results. Working with other Texas IAF groups, Valley Interfaith organized busloads of parishioners to make the long drive to Austin in June 1984 to save an ambitious school reform bill (known as House Bill 72) that was in danger of being jettisoned by the House Public Education Committee. Perhaps even more important than saving the bill—which subsequently pumped millions in additional revenues into Valley schools—was reaping the consequences of the improved student-teacher ratio at the lower grades, which resulted in dramatic increases in student achievement in the ensuing years.[18]

Valley Interfaith's early victories in colonias legislation and the reform of school financing established the community organization's credibility as a key player in local politics. Yet as important as successes related to colonias or education were, they must be seen within the context of the larger purpose of Valley Interfaith, which is leadership development and an expansion of the civic capacity of communities that have historically been disconnected from politics. One important part of this thrust entails the oft-repeated "iron rule"—"Never do for others what they can do for themselves." While the "iron rule" can initially strike observers as a hard-hearted principle, in its essence it is nothing more than an insistence on self-discipline and self-initiated activity in the community-based organizations. "The iron rule doesn't mean that you shouldn't help—or that you don't have an obligation to help—those who truly need it," said Ernie Cortés; "rather, it means that if we really want to develop power, we have to look to ourselves and recognize that if we don't do the work that needs to be done, it won't just happen."[19]

A central part of this organizational emphasis on the iron rule involves the process of discovering talent among those who live and work in poor communities and carefully cultivating it in an explicitly political direction. That talent must entail many different components, such as sensitivity and responsiveness to the needs of the community, relationships with a wide range of community members, an eagerness to learn, and a readiness to demand accountability and public service from political and economic elites. Most concretely, that talent manifests itself in individuals' having a following and having the persuasive ability to bring others to the house meetings, research actions, and accountability sessions that are the essence of the IAF's model of community organizing.

In addition to the emphasis on the iron rule, one key facet of IAF organizing that can easily be overlooked or underestimated has to do with the organizations' anchoring in religious institutions. Unlike businesses—which can be owned and controlled by individuals who live outside of neighborhoods—churches, temples, and synagogues tend to develop a strong sense of ownership among residents of a given locale. Institutions dominated by professionals—whether hospitals, courts, or schools—can easily marginalize indigenous community residents by utilizing professional expertise to discount the values and culture of a community. In addition, religious institutions speak to an ethical and transcendental dimension of personal and social life that provides a natural bridge into different forms of political action. Finally, religious institutions perdure over time, which means that even if individual clergy or laity move out of town or become disengaged, congregations continue to exist and thus have a permanent presence in a community. For all of these reasons, the Industrial Areas Foundation focuses its talent search on clergy and laity when beginning the process of community organizing.[20]

In the context of the Rio Grande Valley, the Catholic nature of the population deserves special mention in this context. As was the case for waves of Irish, German, Polish, and Italian immigrants in the nineteenth century, the Catholic Church plays a key role in mediating the enculturation process of Mexican immigrants in the United States today. Masses that are served in Spanish; scriptural passages that honor work, marriage, and family and are reflected upon in Bible study groups; and specific cultural rituals (such as the *quinceañera*, a coming-of-age celebration for fifteen-year-old girls) or saints that reflect the spirituality of indigenous peoples (such as the Virgin of Guadalupe) provide bridging symbols and ceremonies that enable social cohesion and a sense of belonging in immigrant communities even when households are Spanish monolingual and marginalized from mainstream North American institutions. By anchoring its organizing work in the Catholic Church, Valley Interfaith developed a political base in the most powerful secondary association in the Rio Grande Valley, and one that provided a rich nexus of symbolism, liturgy, and social cohesion for the Lower Border population.

Once Ernie Cortés had laid the groundwork for Valley Interfaith and had initiated work in improving colonias, school reform, and leadership development, he hired Jim Drake, a minister who had years of experience working with César Chávez and the United Farm Workers

Union in California, Arizona, and Texas, to become the lead organizer for the group. Like Cortés, Drake had worked on the failed Starr County strike in 1965, and at one point when Drake and other UFW leaders were arrested for violating a strike injunction, Cortés actually gathered the bond to release the group from jail. Like Cortés, Drake had left the Valley after the Starr County strike with a feeling of anger and resentment toward the Anglo elite that dominated Valley politics. Together Cortés and Drake would work to lay the foundation for a powerful new kind of grassroots organization in the Rio Grande Valley.

In their activities, Cortés and Drake discovered many potential leaders throughout the Valley; working through the parishes, they identified a particular strength in Mexican American women who played leadership roles in their congregations. One example of an early leader that Cortés found was Carmen Anaya. Anaya was born in Monterrey, Mexico; she always loved school and when she was old enough, she studied to become a teacher. In January 1950 she married José Anaya, an American with a vast farm in Hidalgo County that grew tomatoes, sugar beets, chilies, carrots, and lettuce. Her husband's farm stretched over five hundred acres and employed three hundred braceros, or Mexican immigrant laborers, at its peak. In 1951, however, the Anayas lost an estimated $100,000 through a bitter freeze that decimated their crops. Soon thereafter the Internal Revenue Service collected over $20,000 in back taxes. Throughout the 1950s the braceros left and so much land was sold that by 1962 the family was compelled to turn to migrant labor. With six children in tow, José and Carmen harvested crops in California, Idaho, North Dakota, Michigan, and Ohio for close to two decades—an especially arduous task for José, who had had his right leg amputated due to a childhood accident. "Recibimos muchos humillaciones de los anglos porque fuimos mexicanos [We were often humiliated by the Anglos because we were Mexicans]," Carmen Anaya recalled bitterly. "Fue muy feo [It was very ugly]." She knew that it was difficult for the children when they had to be taken out of school in March and when they reentered it in October, and she was angered when her children reported that their teachers hit them at school when they spoke in Spanish. At the same time that the schools were insensitive to the children's linguistic heritage, Carmen swore that they would escape the harsh life of migrant laborers, and education seemed to be the greatest vehicle to security. "Mis hijos van a estudiar [My children are going to study]," she pledged to herself. "Mis hijos se van a educar [My children are going to be educated]." In spite of their meager financial resources, Carmen and

José purchased a full set of encyclopedias for the children, and when the children were older, they would fly them back home to Texas from California before the crops were all gathered so that they could start school on time and be assured of a high school graduation.[21]

Carmen Anaya and her family returned to the Valley to settle permanently in 1979, ending seventeen years of following the crops. José opened a general store in an impoverished colonia known as Las Milpas, and Carmen became active in her local church, Nuestro Señor Catholic Mission, leading prayer groups and assisting in the services. Detecting in Carmen a quick intelligence, a willingness to study hard, and a profound religious faith, the priests in her community invited her to attend a series of training workshops that would help her to understand the theological basis of community organizing.

Carmen Anaya never intended to become politically active; her world was largely shaped by her household, financial constraints, and congregation. She loved reading scripture and was especially moved by Christ's Sermon on the Mount, to which she turned when seeking the solace of faith and guidance for right conduct. But the squalor of her colonia—the unpaved roads, the open sewer lines, and the absence of water from the homes in the sweltering summer months—all grated on her sense of fairness and seemed to be a violation of Christ's injunction to care for the needy. She grew angry at the daily spectacle of children from Las Milpas lining up at the store spigot to carry water in buckets to their homes, and she knew that the heavy rainstorms that often move through the Valley carried the sewage from the outhouses up into backyards where children suffered from infectious diseases at much higher incidences than in other parts of the country. Ernie Cortés felt that Carmen was a woman who would be willing to speak up for her community, who had the anger and the tenacity to challenge politicians and to garner the resources that could improve the conditions in Las Milpas.

Carmen Anaya agreed with Cortés' assessment. "No tengo miedo decir la verdad [I'm not afraid to tell the truth]," she said. "Tengo atrevida." "Atrevida," or boldness, was the aptitude that enabled Carmen to work with other Valley Interfaith leaders and to organize visits to Las Milpas for Governor Mark White, Lieutenant Governor Hobby, Treasurer Ann Richards, and Attorney General Jim Maddox. She would not refrain from pointing out that their expensive shoes had become covered with mud from the unpaved roads, or from asking them whether they were ashamed that children were growing up without running water and with outhouses in their backyards in the United States in the 1980s. Ann

Richards was instantly smitten with Anaya. "Las Milpas was the first colonia that I visited in the Valley," she recalled, "and I liked Mrs. Anaya right away, because there is a genuineness to her that makes her the kind of person that you really like to work with. And the conditions that she shared with us were outrageous. Las Milpas was a trap for people desperately wanting to own their own property who had been taken advantage of by developers who were willing to take advantage of the poorest of the poor."[22]

In her advocacy for the residents of colonias, Carmen Anaya would brook no slights to their dignity. In one famous incident, Anaya had invited Texas state senator Hector Uribe to a Valley Interfaith meeting, and when he arrived in casual dress and without a tie, she insisted that he put a tie on just as he would do if he were meeting with business leaders. And in spite of her inability to speak English, she felt empowered as officials in Austin and the Valley began acting; throughout the second half of the 1980s, the Texas state legislature approved millions of dollars in funds to provide water, drainage, and paved roads to the colonias along the Lower Border.[23]

Cortés and Drake combed the Valley searching out potential leaders like Carmen Anaya who were impatient with the poverty in their neighborhoods and willing to take some risks to effect change. A host of other leaders emerged, such as Esmerejildo Ramos, Ofelia de los Santos, Elisabeth Valdez, Father Leo Ferreira, Elida Bocanegra, Father Alfonso Guevara, Father Jerry Frank, Father Armand Matthew, and Javier Parra. Utilizing the network of parish churches, Valley residents began to learn about a politically nonpartisan strategy for cultivating local leadership. Curious citizens and immigrants attended small meetings in the homes of their neighbors or in their churches or missions to discuss the gravity of their problems and to seek to develop tactics for alleviating the worst manifestations of poverty in the Valley. Some of the sessions were primarily opportunities for organizers like Drake and Cortés to listen to the sentiments of the community; others were structured workshops at which organizers taught Valley residents about the intricacies of school finance and potential strategies they could use to improve their communities. Emboldened by their clergy and parish leaders, citizens and immigrants attended mass Valley Interfaith conventions in locations such as the Mercedes Livestock Show and the Catholic War Veterans Hall in Weslaco, where they challenged public leaders to improve the conditions in the colonias, clean up toxic waste, and improve indigent health care. Known in IAF nomenclature as "accountability sessions," these conventions provided opportunities for local leaders to meet with public officials, demonstrate their leadership through disciplined public speaking, and assure that their elected officials were indeed fulfilling their roles as public servants.

Through all of this activity individuals' perceptions of themselves and their communities slowly began to change. "In the beginning I would get nervous to stand in front of people and talk about issues," Javier Parra recalled. "My knees would shake and my voice would shake. I will never forget this stage in my life. Gradually I got more confident speaking in front of people and I remember meeting with Ann Richards and looking at her at the same eye level and saying, 'Hey, we've got some real issues here in our community.' I'll never forget this. And I have to say that I didn't do it all by myself, but with my priest at Immaculate Conception, and with the support of Bishop Fitzpatrick and all of my peers in Brownsville and McAllen and Harlingen who kept giving me the encouragement and teaching me that I could grow stronger."[24]

Between the small meetings and the much larger conventions, a host of minor events, often reflecting indigenous Mexicanist customs, graced the development of political power with a theological dimension. In December 1985, Carmen Anaya and other local leaders from Las Milpas led a pilgrimage from Nuestro Señor Catholic Church along Highway 281 north to the San Juan Catholic Shrine in Pharr, where a special Mass was held in preparation for a meeting with Lieutenant Governor Hobby to ask for funds for colonia improvement. When Hobby responded with a promise to raise $100 million for a colonia improvement fund and another $100 million for a venture capital fund to increase jobs in the Valley, citizens and immigrants began believing that they could effect change if they organized themselves politically. In a very real sense, they were learning the tools of democracy and acquiring new political identities.

Although some politicians worked well with Valley Interfaith, and many from both sides of the political spectrum welcomed the new emphasis on accountability, others were alienated by the organization. One of the early and most vocal critics of the group was Othal Brand, the mayor of McAllen. "There's not much question their basic philosophy is basically a communistic philosophy," he once told a *New York Times* reporter. Brand particularly detested the accountability sessions. "It never seemed right to me that I or other elected officials should have to get up in front of our constituents and follow a script written out by Valley Interfaith," Brand protested. "Those accountability sessions never give anybody a chance to explain why they have a position. It's just set up to put a lot of pressure on you to agree with whatever Valley Interfaith wants." Beyond the procedural criticism, Brand harbored long-standing personal animosities; when Jim Drake and his UFW colleagues had been arrested by Texas Rangers in the failed Starr County strike, they were on a lettuce and melon ranch owned by Brand called "Trophy." (In addition to his South Texas ranch, Brand also operated vast plantations in Honduras, Guatemala, and El Salvador, where his authoritarian managerial style was exposed in an NBC *Today Show* analysis in 1986.) Brand did not remember the UFW strikers as heroic combatants for social justice, but as lawbreakers who spread nails in front of his workers' tractor tires and poured sugar into the gas tanks of his farm equipment. When Jim Drake was the lead organizer for Valley Interfaith he got back at Brand by refusing to invite him to the group's founding convention while including virtually every other local politician of real prominence—including Governor White—on the stage. Years of mistrust between Valley Interfaith and Brand followed until Brand was finally deposed in 1997. At that time the city's first Mexican American mayor and a former Raza Unida activist, Leo Montalvo, was elected.[25]

It should be noted that although Brand was particularly outspoken in his criticisms of Valley Interfaith, he was not alone, especially in regard to the strategies used in accountability sessions. Norberto Salinas, a Hidalgo County commissioner in the late 1980s, also found the lack of opportunity to express his ideas in such sessions aggravating. In one session in February 1989 Salinas was queried by Carmen Anaya, but interrupted by Amalia Lerma, a Valley Interfaith board member, when he sought to explain how his own position on funding for improving colonias differed from that of Valley Interfaith. "You won't let me talk to the people," he complained. "If you won't let me talk, then don't invite me!"[26]

Occasionally, critics charged that Valley Interfaith organizers were too manipulative in their relationships with the leaders. Eloy Aguilar, the president of a South McAllen neighborhood organization, worked with Valley Interfaith for several years in the 1980s but left it because he felt stifled by the organizers. "They prepare everything for you," he charged, including the wording of the questions leaders were to direct to public officials at accountability sessions. "You couldn't talk or give opinions."[27]

The most vocal antagonist of Valley Interfaith was Tom Pauken, chair of the Texas Republican Party. Pauken was the director of

ACTION in the Reagan administration and oversaw numerous domestic service programs. Pauken's first contact with Valley Interfaith occurred after a freeze in the Rio Grande Valley in December 1983 which decimated the Valley's citrus and vegetable industries and destroyed over 15,000 seasonal jobs. Farmworkers and their families were desperate in the wake of the freeze. There was virtually no commercial citrus production in the Valley that year, and fewer than half of the 69,000 acres in the Valley dedicated to orange and grapefruit production survived the freeze with the prospect of productivity in future years.

Given the economic crisis, in which impoverished farmworkers lost all hope of employment in the winter of 1983–84, Valley Interfaith leaders and organizers began working with the Federal Emergency Management Agency (FEMA) and the Texas Department of Agriculture to assemble an extensive public works program for unemployed farmworkers in the Valley. The leadership of Valley Interfaith hoped that if the farmworkers could receive federal and state compensation for work improving road conditions and the installation of water and sewer lines in poor neighborhoods, then the farmworkers could survive the crisis. Together with FEMA officials, Valley Interfaith elaborated a proposal to direct $66 million to public works projects that would employ 18,000 campesinos in the Lower Border. The proposal was endorsed by the mayors of Hidalgo, La Joya, Brownsville, San Juan, Mission, Alamo, Pharr, Elsa, Edcouch, Alton, and La Villa. Even though Othal Brand refused to endorse the proposal, three of his city commissioners did, fearing that McAllen might lose out on coveted federal dollars due to the intransigence of the mayor.[28]

After convening hundreds of house and parish meetings in the Valley, Valley Interfaith leaders were stunned when Pauken intervened and persuaded President Reagan to empower him to address the crisis in the Valley through a group he created called the "Valley Action Committee" rather than through the proposal Valley Interfaith and FEMA had developed. Working with Valley business leaders such as Joe Chapa and Pete Diaz Jr., Pauken began developing a proposal that would channel federal dollars to the Small Business Administration and the Farmers Home Administration to address the crisis.[29]

The result was a series of angry confrontations between Pauken and Valley Interfaith leaders in March 1984. Valley Interfaith leaders and organizers were infuriated when Pauken scuttled their negotiations with FEMA and began developing alternative policies with ACTION. Ernie Cortés worked quickly behind the scenes to rally all of the Catholic bishops in Texas, who sent letters to the White House in support of Valley Interfaith's initiative and denouncing Pauken's intervention. "That was a real test of Bishop Fitzpatrick's leadership," Cortés recalled, "because he could have just said that Pauken was a Catholic, too, and that he had to be the bishop of all of the people and not just of the poor. Instead, he stood with us and made it clear that you sometimes have to make a choice between the rich and the poor, and that his stance as a church leader was going to be with the poor."[30]

In spite of the public outcry and the bishops' support, the public works proposal developed by Valley Interfaith was not funded. Pauken denounced the proposal and Bishop Fitzpatrick's support of it: "Bishops aren't always right," he said. "This business of pushing down people's throats things like Valley Interfaith is inappropriate for a bishop." Destitute farmworkers only made it through the winter through heavy reliance on soup kitchens developed under local church auspices in the colonias, with some assistance from ACTION.[31]

An even worse problem for Valley Interfaith was that the blowup with Pauken had serious political consequences. Many members of congregations disliked the political dimension that their churches were acquiring through the work of Valley Interfaith, and some began leaving their congregations because of the association. El Divino Redentor Methodist Church in McAllen, Saint Anthony's Catholic Church in Harlingen, and Christ the King Church in Brownsville all stopped paying dues in the months following the Pauken controversy, although Christ the King resumed its membership after a brief hiatus. At the end of 1984 only one Protestant congregation—La Iglesia Metodista Unida in McAllen—remained a dues-paying member.[32]

In addition, conservative Catholics worried that Valley Interfaith was entangling the Church in political matters that fell outside of the Church's sphere of legitimate influence. Pauken himself went on to become a long-standing and outspoken critic of Valley Interfaith and published a book called *The Thirty Years War* in which he denounced the group as a "classic example of a New Left organization" that practiced "confrontational tactics" to advance its interests. "They're smart politically," Pauken told me, "and Ernie Cortés is a brilliant guy, but they have a way of running over people and especially people who don't agree with their agenda. But the best evidence that their kind of politics doesn't work was that Ronald Reagan carried Cameron County in [the presidential election of] 1984 and almost carried Hidalgo County." Since Pauken's confrontation with Valley Interfaith occurred in March and the election was held in November, he reasoned that there was no major fallout for the Republicans from the way he handled the freeze.[33]

It is important to note that from the outset Valley Interfaith was opposed not only by the political elite of the Republican Party, but also by local citizens from the middle and working classes. A group calling itself Concerned Citizens for Church and Country demonstrated outside many of Valley Interfaith's early accountability sessions. The president of the group, Mike Rodriguez, who hailed from La Feria, said, "What we really object to is the idea that they want to use church structures to propagate a new form of political power, a new political base. They are going after that power vacuum that now exists among the poor in the Valley." A similar group based in Harlingen, called the Concerned Citizen's Committee of the Rio Grande Valley, and headed by J. M. Rodriguez, published a leaflet entitled "A Second Look at Valley Interfaith," in the summer after the freeze. The pamphlet charged that "the real purpose of Valley Interfaith is to establish a revolutionary political base under the cloak of the churches," and stated that "if we are to preserve our democratic way of life, we must work together now to get the Marxist octopus of Valley Interfaith off the backs of our elected officials!" Even though the pamphlet freely engaged in the use of hyperbole, it is not clear that all of the members of the Harlingen-based group were unprincipled. Many appear to have agreed with the sentiments of Joe King, a printer from Brownsville, who simply said: "I don't think the church should have a political agenda," and worried about maintaining a firm separation between church and state.[34]

It seems inevitable that there will be some controversy and debate surrounding any community-based organization that combines religious institutions with political power. Valley Interfaith might well benefit from heeding some of the more salient criticisms. In particular, IAF organizations such as Valley Interfaith have been criticized for years for the nature of their accountability sessions. During these meetings, politicians are frequently allowed only one minute to express their response to the organization's agenda. From Valley Interfaith's perspective, the purpose of an accountability session is to demonstrate the power of the organization and not the subtleties of an issue. Nonetheless, it seems inevitable that such a strictly delimited exchange is likely to generate ill will among some public officials, as well as perhaps misrepresenting the give-and-take nature of political processes to the public.

In spite of the criticisms expressed above, many observers are unabashed in their admiration for Valley Interfaith. Although he was at first reluctant to meet with Valley Interfaith when he was the chair of SCOPE, Ross Perot was impressed by the group's organization of a massive accountability session he attended at the Catholic War Veterans Hall in Weslaco in November 1983. His subsequent work with the organization led him to concede, "They're the kind of people you need to accomplish things like major changes in the public schools." Even more than Perot, Ann Richards and Bill Hobby, the Democratic governor and lieutenant governor of Texas, respectively, became outspoken admirers of Valley Interfaith and champions of IAF groups throughout Texas. "I remember the first time I went to Las Milpas," Hobby recalled, "and I saw the raw sewage in the ditches by the side of the dirt roads, and I knew that was why the kids were always getting sick and missing out on their schooling. I knew I had to do something about that." Valley Interfaith leaders especially bristle at the suggestion that they might somehow be pawns in the hands of the organizers. When I asked whether one leader ever felt manipulated by organizers, she responded with indignation. "I'm an intelligent woman," she said. "*Nobody* tells me what to do. If I disagree with an organizer, I say so. And don't forget," she continued, "the leaders pay the organizers, and we can always throw them out if we don't like them. So how are they going to tell us what to do?"[35]

Valley Interfaith's champions tend to see any disagreements between organizers and leaders, or between leaders and critics, as simply part of the rough-and-tumble world of politics, and not as any expression of a unique disability pertaining to the political association. In addition, they see Valley Interfaith as fulfilling a unique need for a political voice for the working poor in the Valley, a powerful, sustained voice that no other organization possesses. "The reality of the matter," Richards said, "is that if you don't have money and are a migrant farmworker from a place like the Valley, you have no voice at all if you don't have a community-based organization like Valley Interfaith." In the 1990s even Senator Kay Bailey Hutchison and Governor George W. Bush—Republicans who ordinarily kept their distance from organizations with even the faintest aroma of radicalism—both came on board and supported Valley Interfaith's continuing agenda for infrastructural improvements in the colonias.[36]

Although political controversy has accompanied much of Valley Interfaith's work, in a broader sense the organization is just as educational as it is political. "Valley Interfaith es para mi como una universidad [Valley Interfaith is like a university for me]," Carmen Anaya said, and her concern is just as much for human development in her colonia as it is for material improvements. True to the IAF's emphasis on broad leadership development, Valley Interfaith held a series of three-day weekend retreats throughout the 1980s and 1990s in San Juan, Harlingen, and South Padre Island where workshop leaders selected passages from scripture dealing with social justice and interpreted Valley Interfaith's organizing efforts in the light of them. In 1985 alone more than 1,500 Valley residents met on six consecutive Sundays for four-hour study groups that discussed the American Catholic Bishops' Letter on the Economy and Pope John Paul's encyclical on work. Those texts, which address social justice issues in the context of Catholic theology, enabled Valley Interfaith leaders to reflect on the troubling winter of the freeze and the ensuing Pauken debacle within a larger spiritual context. In addition, the dialogue that characterized those workshops led to a further course of action to improve Texas' system of indigent care. That effort led to the first undertaking in the state's history to provide comprehensive health service to the poor rather than the piecemeal and fragmented approach that had prevailed in the past.[37]

Achievements such as the state's indigent health care package, colonias legislation, and school-finance reform make it difficult to dismiss Valley Interfaith as diabolical or Machiavellian. Indeed, as the years have passed, the organization has become increasingly well integrated into the politics of the Rio Grande Valley—so much so that some activists worry that it may have inadvertently become part of the status quo. Thus, Valley Interfaith's support for an increase in the sales tax in McAllen in 1997 can be seen as part of a heroic effort of a group to generate additional public revenues for pressing needs; or it can be seen as co-opted participation in a highly regressive money-raising venture with very uncertain outcomes for the poorest citizens and immigrants. The organization is evolving in a complex and multifaceted way, and cannot be encapsulated in simplistic characterizations.

In many ways, the very institutional structure of Valley Interfaith contributes to its enigmatic status. For while Valley Interfaith can easily turn out thousands of participants for accountability sessions, and while the organization can rightfully claim that it has played a leadership role in bringing millions of dollars of federal and state aid to the Valley, it is rarely clear just how broadly based and just how committed the membership is. At times, the organization appears to consist of nothing more than a half dozen overworked organizers operating out of a modest storefront office in downtown Mercedes; yet, like a truly mass organization, it can pack the Field House at the University of Texas Pan American campus in Edinburg on an annual basis and has successfully persuaded public officials to commit to its agenda. On the one hand, it can seem to be deeply woven into the liturgical culture of a church such as Saint Joseph's the Worker in McAllen; on the other hand, it can seem to be an almost empty formality in other churches which do little beyond paying their dues to the organization. In other words, the topography of leaders, institutional bases, and relationships that sustain Valley Interfaith are an ever-changing mosaic, one that responds flexibly to meet the changing needs of Valley residents.

In reviewing the evolution of Valley Interfaith one should keep in mind that the organization has both contributed to and benefited from a growing statewide network of community organizations affiliated with the Industrial Areas Foundation. By the turn of the century the Texas IAF had twelve organizations scattered throughout Texas, from El Paso in the west to Beaumont and Port Arthur in the east, as well as from Dallas Area Interfaith and Allied Communities of Tarrant in the north to the Border Organization (in Laredo) and Valley Interfaith in the Lower Border region. Although Valley Interfaith has very much sought to respond first and foremost to the needs of citizens and immigrants in the Valley, organizers and leaders have also argued that only statewide alliances will allow poor and working-class Valley residents to develop a constituency to create meaningful change on behalf of children and families. The formation of social capital, by means of horizontal ties across the state's most disparate regions and cultures, has thus played a continual role in the evolving culture and politics of Valley Interfaith.

CHAPTER TWO

PARENTAL ENGAGEMENT AT PALMER ELEMENTARY SCHOOL

As noted above, much of the early work of Valley Interfaith focused on improving conditions in the colonias, where concentrated poverty, poor housing conditions, and public health problems were most in evidence. Yet the problems of the colonias were scarcely contained within their geographical boundaries. Their impact was felt throughout all the Valley, affecting the ability of hospitals to serve their clients, schools to teach children, and employers to find skilled labor. For years teachers in the public schools had fretted over the conditions in the colonias; they knew that many of their students were growing up in unsanitary conditions while their parents tried to wrest a living from jobs paying the minimum wage or in the case of *indocumentados,* even less. Yet most teachers tolerated the conditions because they could not discover a means to transform them.

Some educators, however, took an early interest in the initial organizing efforts of Valley Interfaith. One such figure was Salvador Flores, a new principal at Palmer Elementary School in Pharr. Flores' school served children from Las Milpas and many other colonias located south of Pharr along Highway 281. Many of the children from the colonias came to school muddy when it rained; others came with their clothes dirty because their homes did not have water; some would not come at all when their buses could not reach homes over unpaved, rain-soaked roads. (Pharr is little more than one hundred feet above sea level, and because groundwater in the region is close to the surface, paved roads and excellent drainage are crucial to ensure safe transportation.) "I saw the great need that the children had," Flores recalled. "When it rained, many of the kids were absent, because the school buses couldn't get through, or they would walk to school and be all muddy."[1]

Flores had learned of the work of Valley Interfaith from Esmere-jildo Ramos, a fellow parishioner at his church, Saint Margaret's Catholic Church in Pharr. Ramos had years of social activism behind him. He was a former farmworker, citrus fruit packer, and veteran of the Korean War who had worked with the United Farm Workers on the Starr County strike. Inspired by the ministry of Father Alfonso Guevara at Saint Margaret's, he always sought to "help out the guys at the bottom who have no education." Ramos recalled that he recruited members into Valley Interfaith "just through friendship alone"; so since Salvador Flores was a friend, he invited Flores to one of the first accountability sessions. Flores was impressed when he found himself among six thousand other Valley residents at the assembly in McAllen, in which Governor Mark White pledged to support the Valley Interfaith agenda for colonia improvement and the equalization of school funding. "From the very beginning I knew that Valley Interfaith was something good that was going to help the community," Flores said. "That's why I got involved."[2]

Salvador Flores himself was no stranger to poverty. His father was a Mexican vaquero, or cowboy, who had married an American and settled in the small Texas town of Zapata, near Laredo. When his parents turned to migrant labor to earn their living, Flores followed along, leaving school each April and returning in late November. As a child, he had experienced first hand the incongruence between his work helping to support his family and schools in Zapata. "When I returned from picking the crops," he said, "I often found myself taking a test on the material the other children had covered during the previous weeks on the first day I was back in school. They didn't cut me one ounce of slack." Animated by his mother's concern that he find his way to a better life, however, he worked hard in school, did well, and eventually decided to become a teacher. He began teaching in 1965 and became the principal of Palmer in 1982.[3]

Salvador Flores is soft-spoken and rarely seeks the limelight for himself. "I don't like to do too much work in front of large crowds," he said. "I feel much more comfortable helping in the background and working with others to develop their abilities." When Valley Interfaith sent busloads of Valley residents to Austin in 1984 to petition legislators to support the equalization of school funding, Flores went with his parents and teachers and pounded the hallways of the capitol, buttonholing representatives and winning a decisive legislative battle that brought over $212 million of additional state funding to Valley schools. Although community organizations such as Valley Interfaith have never received the recognition they deserve for this work—indeed, the laurels usually go to business leaders—subsequent research has demonstrated that their reforms have resulted in dramatic improvements in the education of children in Texas, particularly through preschool programs for children from low-income families and reductions in the class size of children in the early primary grades.[4]

Because of his work in Palmer Elementary, Flores had constant contact with the realities of poverty in his community; indeed, his school district had the highest percentage of low-income students of any district with more than ten thousand students in the entire state of Texas in the mid-1980s. Concerned about his pupils' well-being, intrigued by the new kind of community empowerment represented by Valley Interfaith, and tenacious in his regular attendance and participation in Interfaith meetings, Salvador Flores soon emerged as an educational leader in the organization. In spite of his circumspect style— or perhaps because of it—the community organizers decided to push him to develop his own political capacity. "I had really enjoyed the mix of people that came together in the Valley Interfaith actions," Flores said, "It was the only place where I saw professionals, farmworkers, and housewives all working together. And I guess it was only natural that after a while the organizers would want me to become more visible." Specifically, Sister Christine Stephens—who became the lead organizer after the departure of Cortés and Drake—asked Flores to question Lieutenant Governor Bill Hobby during the assembly in December 1985. Flores agreed, and subsequently received Hobby's endorsement of Valley Interfaith's agenda.[5]

Flores continued to work with Valley Interfaith on a host of actions, and he took pride in the growth of the organization, which garnered the support of thirty-four dues-paying churches by 1987. In the summer of 1990 he attended a two-week national training institute held in Los Angeles by the IAF's national staff. Soon after Flores returned he joined the executive committee of Valley Interfaith. He was developing the role of the principalship beyond that of the director of a school and into that of a genuine community leader.

When Salvador Flores first came to Palmer as its principal, there was little to distinguish it from any other rural school in a predominantly low-income community in the Valley. Palmer had been founded in 1948 as Thomas Edison Junior High School; like other schools in the district, such as Benjamin Franklin and Henry Ford, it was named after a famous inventor who should inspire students through his example.

In 1980, however, a longtime secretary of the school district named Geraldine Palmer retired, and she had won such a place in the community's heart over the years that it supported a movement to rename Edison in her honor. Today it is a small and seemingly inauspicious school with 32 teachers and a student enrollment of 450 children from kindergarten through the fifth grade. Of the students attending Palmer, 86 percent are classified as economically disadvantaged, and 58 percent have limited English proficiency.

The most striking feature of Palmer that Flores, his teachers, and the community's parents have developed is its strategy for community engagement. Throughout the 1980s Flores worked hard with Valley Interfaith to improve conditions in the colonias in which Palmer's children lived, but there was no direct linkage between the culture of the school and that of the community. In 1991, however, a Valley Interfaith organizer, Jessica Whales, worked with Flores to stimulate new kinds of connections between Palmer and its colonias. Whales devoted a tremendous amount of time to visiting parents in their homes and leading workshops at the school. She received district support for fostering a deeper school-community linkage. "Jessica was instrumental," Flores recalled. Whales understood that if Palmer Elementary School was to win the trust of the parents, teachers would need to redefine their roles and break out of the self-imposed boundaries that fragmented the learning that occurs in school from the home life of the child. Whales was particularly successful at encouraging the teachers to make home visits to learn about parents' concerns and to discuss their children's academic progress. Although some teachers were initially cautious, or even opposed to those visits, others viewed the visits as promising a new opportunity to understand the children better and to form common ties with parents.[6]

Supported by Flores and Whales, Palmer's teachers began making their first home visits in the fall of 1991. These initial trips were not always easy. "When we first started doing our home visits, some of the teachers would come back to the school crying when they saw the conditions that the children were living in," Flores said. Many others were pleased with the warm reception the parents had prepared for them, with special offerings of homemade tamales or cakes; some students had especially arranged their bedrooms and were eager to show them off to their teachers. For the most part, teachers reported a greater sense of reality and compassion for the children, and they became aware that while some children lived in secure middle-class homes, others were moving from one dilapidated shack to another as they were repeatedly evicted due to their inability to pay the rent.[7]

Part of the importance of the home visits involves the cultural chasm that can exist between Hispanic parents and schools. Speaking Spanish at school outside of Spanish-language classes was illegal in Texas until 1969, and many parents have memories of being beaten or having paper towels stuffed in their mouths by teachers for using their native tongue. Few parents in colonias experienced success in school themselves, and many are painfully aware of their lack of education. Finally, *indocumentados* are concerned that individuals in positions of authority such as teachers can ascertain their illegal status and will report them to the Immigration and Naturalization Service (INS).

Palmer Elementary School was not alone in exploring a heightened level of school and community collaboration in the early 1990s. Throughout Texas in the early 1980s, educators such as Salvador Flores and community leaders such as Carmen Anaya had battled successfully with IAF community organizations, the League of United Latin American Citizens, and the Mexican American Legal Defense and Education Fund to improve funding for the state's poorest school districts. After legislation addressing this issue was secured in 1984, sister IAF organizations to Valley Interfaith launched school and community collaborations that improved schools that had been struggling for years to enhance academic achievement. In Fort Worth, Morningside Middle School collaborated with the Allied Communities of Tarrant (ACT) in the late 1980s and went from rock-bottom achievement on the state's standardized test to third place among twenty middle schools in the city in just two years. In Houston, Jefferson Davis High School began a similar partnership with The Metropolitan Organization at roughly the same time, and as the parents became more involved, the school was able to cultivate a powerful collaboration with the Tenneco Corporation that contributed to the college expenses of many inner-city and immigrant youths. Similar partnerships blossomed in El Paso, Austin, and San Antonio in the early 1990s. In each instance, home visits by teachers and members of community-based organizations—such as those initiated at Palmer by Jessica Whales—provided a key transition to changing the culture of the school from one of bureaucratic isolation to civic engagement and joint deliberation about the status of children in a community.[8]

By 1992 IAF organizations in Texas had developed enough power and credibility in schools to initiate a network of their own in collaboration with the Texas Education Agency, the state's department of education. Beginning with twenty-one schools, the network of schools —called "Alliance Schools"—granted a number of resources to teachers, students, parents, and community members. They provided badly needed financial capital for the professional development of teachers and innovative programs such as peer mediation and after-school instruction for students. Alliance Schools have also enjoyed a special green-light status for waivers from state and district guidelines; those waivers expedite rapid approval of innovations that could otherwise be stalled by state or district ordinances. The network has connected innovative teachers and principals and concerned parents from throughout Texas with one another, so that reformers can participate in a larger statewide enterprise that will encourage strategic risk-taking, a free exchange of ideas and experiences, and ongoing assessment for Alliance School members. Perhaps most importantly, the Alliance Schools have connected public schools with both religious institutions and the political process, simultaneously rupturing the isolation experienced by many schools and providing them with social capital that can be leveraged to enhance both schools and their surrounding communities.

In October 1991 Ernie Cortés visited Palmer to discuss the possibility of developing a formal collaboration between Valley Interfaith and the elementary school. During the subsequent winter and spring, Palmer's faculty discussed the pros and cons of such a partnership. "That was an issue that took a *lot* of discussion," Salvador Flores recalled, "because there were some real concerns about an organization like Valley Interfaith coming into our school." While the history of collaboration with Valley Interfaith had been appreciated by the teachers, and Jessica Whales' work was viewed as particularly productive, there was still some concern about what a formalized collaboration might entail. Some teachers were wary of the manner in which Valley Interfaith seemed to mix politics and religion; others saw the partnership as a potential weakening of the boundary that separates church and state; still others were concerned that a partnership with a community organization might compromise their professional autonomy. The issue was particularly vexing because for a school to become an Alliance School, IAF organizations like Valley Interfaith require unanimous support from faculty, fearing that a simple majority vote in favor of the collaboration is not sufficient to really accomplish the cultural transformations that are needed to make schools centers of civic engagement.

In the case of Palmer, the teachers of one grade level were particularly resistant at the outset. When many faculty members attended an educational conference convened by the Industrial Areas Foundation organizations in Texas, however, they returned excited about the potential of a partnership with Valley Interfaith and a broader statewide network of community organizations. Finally, only one faculty member blocked the consensus. "No matter what you say," she told Flores, "I'm not going to change my mind." The potential partnership stalled. "What finally happened," said Flores, "was that I called Valley Interfaith lead organizer Tim McCluskey and told him that we had a holdout, but that everyone else was on board. Tim decided we would go ahead with it."[9]

The first real manifestation of Valley Interfaith's work in the culture of Palmer occurred through the home visits that teachers made to parents. Within a year, however, teachers had begun wondering whether the visits could be improved upon. One major problem was that the visits had to be done on Saturdays, when many teachers felt that they deserved to be off from work. To relieve teachers of this extra time, Palmer developed an alternative strategy in which the school uses its Alliance School funds to pay for substitute teachers, thus enabling all of the teachers in the school to visit all of the students' homes on school days. The visits have been arranged to enable the first grade teachers go on a Monday, the second grade teachers on the following Tuesday, and so forth. The teachers ask the parents for their perceptions of the school, share their initial impressions of the students, invite the parents to upcoming meetings at the school, and ask the parents if they have any ideas about anything that can be done to improve the school. Some of the parents have asked for help when they have problems with their children in the home, and the school has responded by offering parenting sessions in which parents, many of them single mothers, have an opportunity to talk about their difficulties and receive support from their peers. The teachers also use the home visits to recruit parents to help with instruction. "We need the parents in the classrooms," Salvador Flores commented. "That's where they can really be most effective." Almost all of the home visits are conducted in Spanish, which only one teacher at Palmer does not speak. In her case, a parent or another teacher accompanies her to translate.[10]

Following the home visits, Flores has planned a report card night in early October of each year for the parents to come to the school and learn about their child's academic progress. On this evening the teachers try to alert parents early on about any problem areas that the children might be facing with their coursework, and they let the parents know about their goals for the year and strategies that parents can use to help improve their children's learning. Parents are also informed about Texas' standardized test, the Texas Assessment of Academic Skills (TAAS), and are advised that whatever one's beliefs about standardized tests, failure to learn to do well on them can result in their children being tracked to a lower level in secondary school or failing to graduate from high school altogether. Because so many Hispanic youths are tracked to the lowest level in secondary schools, Flores and his staff work hard to follow a districtwide strategy distributing assessment throughout the year so that teachers and parents receive regular opportunities to ascertain just how well their children are learning.

Even if it causes some discomfort among teachers, Flores does not shy away from sharing the test results of the different classes at meetings of the school's campus council. He hopes that the easy access to knowledge and his readiness to discuss discrepancies across classrooms will help create a greater accountability in the school and a greater sense of trust with the community. "We need to ask ourselves questions, and to let ourselves feel some pressure, because our parents want to understand the reasons for the results." Because many parents are dependent on public transportation that runs irregularly in the evening, Flores negotiated successfully with his school board and superintendent to use school buses to pick up parents and take them to and from these meetings.[11]

Palmer's teachers have responded with enthusiasm to the new school culture and the multiple connections to the students' homes. "We want to teach the whole child, and if you want to do that, you really have to visit the homes," one teacher commented. Another teacher said, "In the beginning, I was reluctant to visit the homes. I really didn't see it as part of my job. But the parents have been so responsive, and it has helped me in so many ways in working with the children. Now I don't know how I got by without it before."

"No doubt about it, it's an eye-opener, every time you go for a home visit," one teacher said. "Some parents are so enthusiastic, and they have home-baked goodies all ready for you. Several of my children have just insisted that I see their bedrooms, and set them up with everything just perfectly in its place for me to see. And then there is the other side, where no parents are home, or where you're afraid to even enter their yards, the dogs are so fierce. But either way you learn what the kids are growing up with, and I'll tell you, you also learn to admire the kids, when you see what some of them are up against."

Teachers were asked about their work with Valley Interfaith and whether they felt that the community-based organization had fulfilled its responsibilities in establishing stronger ties with the community. "I had heard criticism of Valley Interfaith before we worked with them, but once you get involved, it's different," one teacher remarked. "They certainly haven't told us how to do our jobs. . . . They let people know that they can do for themselves. When they taught us how to do home visits, they empowered us to do for ourselves."

Encouraged by the growing ties between parents and teachers, Salvador Flores has worked hard to develop a pedagogy of place at Palmer that will honor children's homes and their cultures. As one expression of that respect for the community, Flores and his teachers had a bilingual education program in the school until the mid-1990s. At that time Palmer faculty questioned whether they could develop an instructional program that would not just help Spanish-speaking children make a developmentally appropriate transfer to English in the classroom, but would also help the children maintain and develop their Spanish with the goal of achieving full biliteracy in both languages at the end of the fifth grade. Faculty agreed that Spanish/English biliteracy was an important and obtainable goal, and parents enthusiastically concurred. Since Salvador Flores estimates that roughly 80 percent of the parents are Spanish monolingual—and only one teacher at Palmer is not proficient in Spanish—the decision to develop a dual-language program offered an additional opportunity to draw parents into the school's mission.

Palmer's teachers then began to receive training in the implementation of the two-way dual-language program in 1994 and 1995. The program began in the 1995–96 school year with preschoolers and kindergarteners and will gradually work its way up all of the grade levels. Students at the lower grade levels now receive reading and writing instruction in their native language, whether English or Spanish. They receive math education only in English and science and social studies only in Spanish. Other classroom activities, such as art or circle time, shift from Spanish dominance to English dominance on alternate days of the week.

The implementation of a two-way program requires an intricate and thorough approach to virtually all facets of instruction, curriculum development, and assessment. Morning announcements throughout Palmer and the pledge of allegiance are done in English one day and Spanish the next. Signs on the doorways of each classroom indicate "Please speak English here today" or "Por favor habla español aquí hoy" on alternate days. Students who speak English on a day in which Spanish is dominant are gently encouraged by teachers to try their Spanish, and the reverse occurs on the alternate days. Spanish-dominant students are paired with English-dominant students as partners each week, and the partners rotate throughout the school year. Spanish and English labels are evident throughout the classroom, identifying both objects (computer/computadora) and activities (for example, student art work on a bulletin board underneath a label of "innovation/innovación"). Because language instruction is received in the mother tongue, all students receive ninety minutes of practice with reading and writing each day; teachers combine classes in such a manner that all English-dominant students work with one first grade teacher, for example, while all Spanish-dominant students work with another.

Through his leadership, Salvador Flores has developed Palmer Elementary into a model of community engagement in Hidalgo County. He takes pride in the support of his teachers for the innovations at Palmer, and remarked, "The staff has seen the benefits. We can use Alliance School funds to give them additional training, and they like the support that they get during the parenting sessions. People who come from other schools see the differences and say that they don't see the usual familiar roles on our campus. And the parents see the differences too."[12]

It is worth noting that not all of the achievements at Palmer have been accomplished without friction. In particular, Flores has had to remind Valley Interfaith on occasion that the teachers do not work for the community-based organization, but for Palmer Elementary. Flores once had to go head-to-head with an organizer who called from Harlingen and explained that she was going to be late for a workshop that she had planned to hold for the faculty. "I had to tell her there was no way I was going to hold my faculty until 4:30 to wait until she arrived," Flores said. "I can't do that to my teachers." On another occasion, a Valley Interfaith organizer urged one of Palmer's parent liaisons to develop more of an agitational, community-organizing dimension to her work. Again Flores intervened, reminded the liaison that she worked for Palmer and not Valley Interfaith, and affirmed that there are many different kinds of roles to develop when supporting parents' school engagement. Each of these examples were relatively minor incidents, but they are worth noting as reflections of the challenges that occur when schools and community-based organizations collaborate.[13]

The Alliance School network provides one avenue for educators to learn about successful reforms being implemented by other schools in similar circumstances in their region. By attending Alliance School conferences, Salvador Flores and his staff learned that Alliance Schools in San Antonio had created more than one hundred free after-school programs in schools in the early 1990s. Acutely aware that many children from Palmer arrived at homes without parental supervision when they left school, Flores worked with parents and teachers to create a free after-school program for children, which began in the 1996–97 school year and has continued up to the present. Using Alliance School funds and offering classes in ballet folklórico, computer education, and a host of other activities of high interest to the children, the after-school program enrolled over one-third of all Palmer students and gave them valuable instructional activities until 5:30 each school day.

One popular dictum of IAF organizers is that "all organizing is re-organizing," which is often used to recognize the ongoing and continual nature of community development. One example of this reality concerns the rezoning of neighborhoods in the Pharr–San Juan–Alamo Independent School District, which has been growing rapidly in the last quarter century. In 1996 Palmer lost a colonia known as Hidalgo Park as part of its catchment area; this loss was sorely felt because the neighborhood had been highly organized by Valley Interfaith and contained a rich variety of parent leaders. Instead of Hidalgo Park, the district rezoning sent 152 new children to Palmer from Via del Valle and Siete Encinos colonias. Via del Valle is a particularly impoverished colonia, and while Siete Encinos is brand-new and has some nice homes, many area youth gangs, such as the Tri-City Bombers and the Po' Boys, have strong membership there. Few of the parents of these pupils—who now made up over a third of the student body at Palmer—had experience with Alliance Schools or Valley Interfaith.[14]

To help organize the new neighborhoods, Palmer hired Yolanda Castillo, a parent involvement specialist, in March 1997. In her initial contacts with parents, Castillo experienced "a lot of apathy" among parents, which deeply disturbed her. Yet because of her own background, Castillo knew well about the difficulty that many parents face and their preoccupation with financial matters. Like many of the parents, she herself is an immigrant, having moved to Texas from San Luis Potosí in the interior of Mexico in 1969; also like many parents, she worked for years as a migrant laborer, and only finished following the crops when she graduated from high school. To try to reach out to the parents, Castillo held parent education sessions at Cristo Rey Lutheran Church in the community until she observed that some Catholics believed that they should not enter Protestant churches. Since then the meetings have been moved to parents' homes, and the response has been enthusiastic.[15]

Aside from cultural issues that can create barriers between low-income Mexican American parents and schools, another important reason for educators to shift to community-based activities is that many low-income parents lack reliable means of transportation to attend school meetings. Salvador Flores commented, "It's very difficult for parents to be involved when they're so far away from the school." To help with this problem, Flores was able to work with the district to acquire school buses to take parents to parenting sessions at Palmer.[16]

Many children appear to have benefited from the changes in their school and community. One can hardly question whether the children like their principal; when I first met him after school in March 1997, a little girl was insisting on demonstrating her newly developed reading skills to him, and Flores can hardly take ten steps in the school without flocks of bright-eyed children approaching him with a cascade of enveloping hugs. One child who has especially benefited from Palmer's parental-engagement strategy is Angel Bustos, who, like his mother, Rosario, was raised in Las Milpas. When Rosario grew up in Las Milpas, there was no public provision for sewage and none of the roads were paved. "It was just bad," she recalled. "We had water, but that was about it, and we especially had problems with the flooding of the casitas [outhouses] when it rained. And many of us didn't know that there was anything we could do about it."[17]

Rosario became active in Valley Interfaith when she became a mother and wanted to assure that her children would have a better community to grow up in. She has taken long bus trips to Austin with other Valley Interfaith leaders to meet with political leaders and to fight for funding to improve the schools, roads, and drainage in her community. In the spring of 1997 she took her son with her to a Valley Interfaith meeting with the Texas Water Development Board in Austin to confirm its commitment to an additional $21 million for colonia improvement in the Valley. Angel, then in third grade, read a statement he had prepared with his mother: "We, the children of Las Milpas, can look forward to clean drainage ditches, new sewer drains, and pure drinking water. Thank you for caring about the children of South Texas, because we are the future of Texas."[18]

A parent such as Rosario Bustos views her work as much more multifaceted than purely internal school reform. A reader of the local press, Bustos observed a growing public sentiment that because of the increasing political engagement of Las Milpas, a certain resentment was developing among citizens in more affluent areas who envied the channeling of resources to the colonias, which lie several miles south of the heart of Pharr. Leo Palacios, a city commissioner, commented in an interview published in the *Advance News Journal* in May 1997, "We can't neglect the rest of Pharr in sole favor of Las Milpas. Yes, that area is important, but so is Pharr's old city proper. And what worries me is that some politicians will cater solely to Las Milpas just because they're afraid of losing the two hundred to three hundred votes that the Valley Interfaith folks down there will bring to the polls." Concerned that Pharr's city council would undermine the growing civic engagement of Las Milpas, Rosario Bustos made it a point to speak before the next council meeting on behalf of Valley Interfaith's work there. Accompanied by Eddie Anaya—the son of Carmen and José—and David Perez, a counselor at Palmer, Bustos made sure that the city council appreciated all of the revenues (most of which came from state and federal sources) that Valley Interfaith had brought to both Las Milpas in particular and Pharr in general.[19]

Engagement from parents such as Rosario Bustos is facilitated by the example set by Salvador Flores but also by the continued presence of Valley Interfaith organizers in the school and community. In May 1997, organizer Estela Sosa-Garza provided an overview of Alliance School culture to a roomful of roughly twenty-five parents—all mothers—at Palmer. Speaking in Spanish, Sosa-Garza led the parents through a step-by-step explanation of the underlying principles and organizing framework of the Alliance School effort. She juxtaposed the unilateral nature of many school bureaucracies to the Alliance School attempt to create a culture of collaboration and relational power; she contrasted many schools' disconnectedness from their surrounding communities to the Alliance School emphasis on strong ties between families and schools; and she noted that Alliance Schools do not expect or strive for quick, superficial results but are much more animated by the vision of a "cambio de largo plazo—un cambio cultural [large-scale change—cultural change]." Parents responded well to her presentation, which seemed most important not in terms of the day-to-day culture at Palmer but in terms of understanding that Palmer is part of a larger network of schools throughout Texas that are struggling to become more responsive to and engaged with their surrounding communities.

By the fall of 1997 parents in the school had become used to a high level of advocacy for their children. They had met with assistant superintendents to secure building repairs, portable classrooms, and other infrastructural repairs, and they had organized a community jamaica, or festival, that rallied hundreds of neighborhood residents and featured traditional Mexican dances and a local mariachi group. When two break-ins occurred in the school and more than $3,000 worth of computer equipment was stolen, the parents worked with both the Pharr police and the school district to increase security. A critical mass of parent leaders who no longer waited for the principal to tell them what they needed for a good educational environment had been developed. They were proactive and even aggressive in making sure that the children had all of the ingredients for a positive learning atmosphere at the school. "You tell us what you need, Mr. Flores," one of the parents remarked self-confidently to him. "We'll get it for you."[20]

Through the development of its internal culture since joining the Alliance School network, Palmer has exemplified a key distinction that must be drawn between accommodationist forms of parental *involvement* and transformative kinds of parental *engagement*. Parental involvement is often stressed as an important component of the work of school reform, but most schools enact parent involvement in such a way that parents are relegated to menial tasks such as photocopying, shelving library books, or preparing classroom supplies. Since that work *can* help to enhance the learning environment of children, it should not be disparaged as unimportant. In the work of Alliance Schools, however, one of the key tasks of organizers and leaders is to expand the repertoire of possibilities open to parents so that they can not only support the traditional work of the school but also transform it through civic engagement. To distinguish this second type of more activist community interface from the first, it is useful to designate the second as parental *engagement* to underline its more sustained and radical nature.[21]

Palmer's greatest success in this area in the 1998–99 school year came when parents and teachers united to persuade the school board to build additional classroom space for the preschoolers and kindergarteners and to build a new library facility. Sister Judy Donovan of Valley Interfaith met with groups of teachers at each grade level to discuss strategy, and organizer Carissa Baldwin worked with the parents to conduct research and prepare a compelling case to present to the board. Construction was approved and both projects—including the new, half-million-dollar library—were completed in the fall of 1999.

Important as these successes are, some parents are struggling too much simply to make ends meet to conduct advocacy for the school or community. My most heartrending experience in the Rio Grande Valley concerned a home visit I made with parent liaison Yolanda Castillo to inquire after a troubled student. The student had been bullying his peers and would not stop his physical attacks on them, in spite of the repeated admonitions of his teachers, principal, and Castillo. Upon visiting the home we found the student's mother in a one-room hovel with her few meager possessions heaped upon a filthy mattress. She was an undocumented immigrant and supported herself by selling homemade tamales door to door in Pharr. Her husband had abandoned her and her son and only returned intermittently to threaten her and to demand money. She wept openly and Castillo did her best to offer comfort. Castillo confessed afterward, "I don't know how much longer I can continue to do this work. I see a situation like that and I feel so helpless. No wonder the child is so violent if that's how he's always seeing that his father behaves!" The boy was the only child who came to school on the first day of the following summer vacation—not knowing where else to go or what else to do.[22]

Recognizing the pressures in the community for additional resources and training, faculty and staff at Palmer worked with Stephen Winchester, a Teach for America teacher from another Pharr–San Juan–Alamo district school, to compile a grant proposal that funded another parent liaison staff position and brought in a host of resources for teaching parents English as a Second Language, computer literacy, citizenship classes, and the skills they need to receive general equivalency degrees. The relatively empty classroom where the parents met previously is now filled with books, drill activities that parents can use to reinforce classroom activities at home, and computers. Yolanda Castillo and Salvador Flores hired Iris Urbina to teach the classes, and Susanna Alvarado works with parents and teachers to target those materials that parents can use in tutoring their children in academic skills at home. Castillo and Urbina have new computer-equipped offices in which to work, and parents who have played leadership roles in the school and community are now increasingly visible in classrooms, where they assist with all levels of instruction.

In spite of the many positive developments at Palmer, standardized test scores indicate that there is considerable room for improvement in the arena of students' academic achievement. Before turning to the data, some contextual information is helpful. First, the TAAS test was first administered in Texas schools in 1990; but in 1992 newly appointed Texas Commissioner of Education Lionel (Skip) Meno changed the design of the test, which pupils would take it, and the time of the year it was to be taken. As a result, TAAS scores from 1990 to 1992 and from 1993 to the present cannot be compared.

Second, Palmer Elementary School served only children in the lower grades through the first half of the 1990s, and children from grades three through five attended another nearby neighborhood school. As a consequence, Palmer students first took the TAAS in the 1995–96 academic year. Third, starting in 1997, third grade students who were Spanish language dominant began taking a Spanish-language TAAS measuring reading and mathematical abilities.

Fourth, small numbers of students took these tests at Palmer. On the Spanish-language reading and math tests, for example, only twelve Palmer students took the fifth grade reading and math tests in 1999; if only a few of those students struggle with the tests and have poor results, the percentage of students failing is greatly magnified. Finally, as the preceding narrative indicates, the central office of the Pharr–San Juan–Alamo Independent School District has regularly reassigned students from different neighborhoods to Palmer, so that the student body has not been stable over time, but has changed on an almost annual basis, given the district's shifting school enrollments.

On the whole, the data indicate that Palmer's school reform strategy emphasizing parental engagement is not translating into strong academic gains, at least not as measured by the TAAS. For all of the available TAAS data on Palmer, see the Appendix. Palmer third graders showed a slower rate of progress than students in the district or the state on the reading test, and their math scores show a decline (almost 20%) from 1996 to 1999, as compared to steady gains for the state and virtually no movement in the district. There was little difference between the campus, district, and state gains on the fourth grade reading and mathematics outcomes. Pertaining to mathematics, Palmer fifth graders showed a greater rate of progress than students from the district or the state.

The difficulties in interpreting the TAAS data are evident in the graph shown on page 40. Palmer fifth graders showed modest gains on the reading test from 1996 to 1999. The 1998 testing year was an exception to a pattern of slow progress from 67 percent passing in 1996 to 75 percent passing in 1999. The dip in the number of test-taking students in 1998 (from 45 in 1997 to 36 in 1998) may account for the higher passing rate; it may be that the weaker students were not tested that year. Once the number of test-takers rose back to 46 in 1999, the passing rate

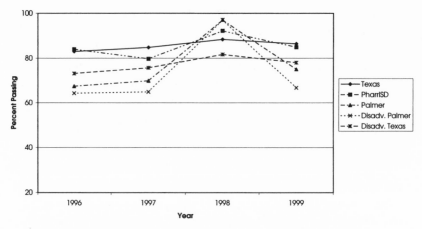

Grade 5 TAAS Reading Test, Palmer Elementary School, 1996–1999.

resumed the pattern of slow and steady growth shown in the chart. One should note that fifth graders indicated even smaller gains for the state and no gains for the district.

On the fourth grade writing tests Palmer's students had high passing percentages for the first three administrations of the TAAS, but the percentage decreased from 1998 to 1999. For the first time, Palmer's disadvantaged students scored below disadvantaged students statewide. It is too soon to know whether the 1999 results are an erratic outlier in a general pattern of strong scores, or whether subsequent scores will indicate a general decline over time.

Given Palmer's emphasis on dual language instruction, one would anticipate that the students would do well on the Spanish-language TAAS test that was introduced in 1997. Here again, however, the results are disappointing. Third graders' rate of progress is lower than that of the district and the state on the reading test and only slightly better than the state (although significantly better than the district) on the math test. Fourth graders made dramatic gains in mathematics from 1997 (at 51.8%) to 1999 (at 91.7%) on the math test, far outpacing the district and the state.

At the fifth grade level Palmer students had trouble with the Spanish-language TAAS. Only 14.3 percent of them passed the reading TAAS in 1999, far below the district (29.1%) and the state (33.5%), although one should note sizable drops in achievement for all groups from the previous year, leading one to wonder whether the new test was more demanding than its predecessor. Palmer fifth graders also performed more poorly than their peers at the state and district level on the Spanish-language mathematics section of the test.

The overall variation in Palmer students' test scores raises a number of questions, none of which have easy answers. Assuming that the test is properly calibrated year after year, what explains the occasionally dramatic transitions in scores on an annual basis? Why has the school struggled to keep up with the rate of gain at the district and state level with respect to outcomes in several of the different categories? To what extent do the low numbers of students or the shifting student populations misrepresent student learning at *this* school?

It is reasonable to suspect that a combination of teacher effects, student effects, and testing effects played a role here. Concerning teacher effects, walk-throughs during on-site visits did not indicate overt problems with instruction. Teachers had planned classes that were focused and well sequenced; students were actively engaged in learning processes; parents played helpful roles as teachers' aides and supplemented instruction with tutorials for children with special needs. It might be the case that so much of the focus of the school's energy has been on parental engagement and the dual language program that students' test-taking skills may not have been emphasized sufficiently.

1998–99 was a heady year for Palmer. A large federal grant was acquired to expand parental engagement, and implementing the grant consumed much of the time of staff that might ordinarily focus their attention more on academics. In addition, the dual language program initiated at the preschool level was only beginning to slowly inch its way up the grade levels, and such programs are notorious for the amount of time they require if they are to be successful.

The struggle to improve TAAS scores has created an opportunity for oppositional teachers to express their misgivings about Palmer's focus on parental engagement. Some teachers have complained about all of the resources going into parent education and have been especially taken aback by the new offices and computer equipment generated by the grant to support that work. When the 1999 TAAS results were reported, the dip in scores brought tears to some teachers' eyes, since they had counted on continued progress with the goal of earning the ranking of an "exemplary" campus by the Texas Education Agency. Instead, Palmer slipped from "recognized" to "acceptable"—a troubling outcome for an Alliance School seeking to create a model of community engagement in the Rio Grande Valley.

Palmer was rezoned again during the summer of 1999, so that

roughly 40 percent of students in the fall came from a new area, Sol Brilla, which now requires a new round of organizing. Salvador Flores intends to hold firm with the civic-engagement strategy that Palmer has developed over the years. He anticipates that TAAS scores will improve as a result of an increased emphasis on test-taking in the classrooms, although he hopes to preserve a balanced instructional approach, including appropriate emphasis on science, the arts, and social studies—domains not measured by the TAAS. Yolanda Castillo plans to persist in her community outreach work, and wants to generate linkages with different job training programs in the Valley. She wants to make sure that parents are not simply educated at Palmer, but that they also learn about employment prospects that will pay a living wage.

In spite of the remaining challenge to improve student achievement as measured by the TAAS, it is nonetheless striking to consider how far Palmer Elementary has come since it became an Alliance School. Parents are organized and are vocal advocates on behalf of the school before the school board. A dual language program to promote Spanish-English biliteracy has been established. Over eighty children attend Palmer from outside of its catchment area on the basis of special requests by parents. Although there have been occasional sources of friction between Valley Interfaith and Palmer, these are inevitable in virtually any relationship and their occasional appearance has occurred in the context of otherwise strong networks of mutual support. Yet such complementary relationships are hardly inevitable—as the following case study will reveal.

CHAPTER THREE

CONTESTED CHANGE AT ALAMO MIDDLE SCHOOL

Palmer Elementary was the first school in the Rio Grande Valley to become an Alliance School and to capitalize on the resources offered by the new venture. Its progression within the network has been relatively frictionless, as teachers and parents have supported one another in joint relationships that aim to improve both the school and the community. Yet because of the smooth and gradual progression of its relationship with the community, Palmer is perhaps atypical.

One school with a more contested history in the Alliance School network is Alamo Middle School, located a few miles east of Palmer on Highway 83 in Alamo. Opened in 1988 to accommodate Alamo's growing population, the middle school was a tough place for students and teachers alike in its first few years. In spite of its sparkling new facilities, gangs dominated the hallways and teachers constantly had to discipline students for food fights, unruly behavior in classrooms, and altercations in restrooms. "It was a zoo," Lesley Whitlock, an assistant principal, recalled. "We had gangs and we had three or four fights going on at once." Frightened by the breakdown in respect for authority, teachers withdrew from one another and focused on their own classrooms. "One of the worst things of that time," one sixth grade teacher remembered, "is that teachers wouldn't support other teachers. A student would cuss you out, or run down the hall, and even if other teachers saw it, they wouldn't say anything." The first principal, Scott Owings, struggled without success at Alamo for two years, at which point the school board decided that a change in leadership was needed.[1]

The school board thought that they found a possible leader for Alamo Middle School in René Ramirez, an assistant principal at Pharr–San Juan–Alamo High School, known in the area simply as "PSJA."

Ramirez had been in charge of discipline at PSJA and had done an effective job. In addition, Ramirez seemed eager to be in charge of a campus, and to expand his leadership beyond simply keeping order in the school.

Like Salvador Flores, Ramirez is an active Catholic who wanted his school to respond to issues that were having an impact on the whole community. As a young man he was an altar boy at Saint John the Baptist in San Juan, where he grew up in the Palma Vista colonia, and he worked with other young people to hold prayer meetings in the various colonias in and around San Juan. "I got close to the people in the community that way," he recalled, "and I thought it would be terrific to be an educator and to find a way to connect the school to the home and the community and to bring everything all together." After graduating from PSJA in 1971, he headed off to college, then returned to teach in his home community in 1975.[2]

In his first year at Alamo, Ramirez made an effort to know the faculty, the students, and the community. He implemented no bold changes, and simply worked on winning the trust of his colleagues and the pupils. Based on his observations, he felt that many changes were needed in the school, but was unsure about which path to change to pursue. As with most middle schools in Texas, classes at Alamo were roughly fifty minutes long and the school was organized around its departments, with different sections of the building devoted to science, social studies, English, and so forth. Orthodox as this arrangement was, it did not appear to be working for the students. Yet which reforms were appropriate?

Recognizing the need for new information, Ramirez formed teams of teachers and parents in his second year that went with him to visit Texas schools that were exploring innovative approaches to instruction, curriculum design, assessment, and community engagement. One school that they visited was J. Frank Dobie Middle School in Austin, which gave them a number of ideas about strategies for transforming the internal culture of Alamo from that of a junior high school to a more age-appropriate middle school concept. Dobie radicalized Ramirez's concept of what needed to be done with Alamo. "When I first got here," he said, "what we really had was a miniature high school. Our layout was just like a high school, with a bunch of different departments scattered around and no one really keeping track of our kids in a way that allowed for any oversight. Our meetings only involved department heads; most of the teachers weren't involved. The whole focus was on the content area.

"But we knew that wasn't working for us. We learned that there was a middle school concept which aimed to do something different: to focus totally on the student." To ensure that Dobie's success was replicable, Ramirez and his colleagues planned another site visit, to Berta Casava Middle School, in nearby San Benito. Just like Dobie, Berta Casava had teams of teachers working closely with students and meeting on a daily basis to discuss difficulties with students, curricular alignment, and the myriad problems that arise as part of the process of teaching young adolescents. Unlike Alamo, at Casava students appeared to be calm, focused on their studies, and respectful. "The whole school atmosphere was different," one teacher recalled. "We saw kids in the hallways who were unsupervised working on projects and they were all under control. They were getting things done and doing fine. At that time that was a foreign concept for us because we still had lots of gang problems. We were wowed!"[3]

Emboldened by the success they witnessed at Dobie and Casava, Ramirez and his colleagues decided to take a risk in the fall of 1993 and try the middle school structure at Alamo. For Ramirez, that meant shifting to a more student-centered organization in which interdisciplinary clusters of teachers would work to get to know students well and would operate through a network of small teams in a common wing of the school. Yet rather than risk a tumultuous reorganization of the entire school at the outset, an experimental cluster would be initiated, and Ramirez found some volunteers who were willing to give it a chance. Among others, teachers Robert Martinez, Ermilia Sanchez, and Darvin Koenig agreed to pilot the concept with a group of 150 students in common.

At roughly the same time that Ramirez and his colleagues made different site visitations, the principal was approached by his superintendent, Ernesto Alvarado, who told him about a new opportunity to develop strong ties to Valley Interfaith and a new network of schools called "Alliance Schools." Ramirez had developed a positive impression of Valley Interfaith and its work with colonias, get-out-the-vote drives, and health care issues. "I was so excited by my first contacts with Valley Interfaith," he recalled. "I wanted people in our community to understand what was happening inside our school. I wanted them to come and to ask us what we were doing for our migrant laborers, for our immigrants, and for our gifted and talented. We know that without a good parental involvement program in our school, we're not going to get the success that we need. I'd like to fill up the cafeteria with parents when we have PTO meetings. I envision parents in the classroom. I envision parents monitoring the hallways." Regrettably, when Jessica Whales—who had successfully worked with Palmer—made her first presentation on behalf of Valley Interfaith, many teachers felt threatened by the tone of urgency she brought to their meeting. "Jessica frightened us because she was very aggressive in a not very mexicana way," one teacher recalled. "We weren't used to that." Another teacher recalled, "I was opposed to the collaboration with Valley Interfaith from the start, and it was because I was concerned about the separation of church and state."[4]

While Whales' approach may have been more strident at Alamo, and issues concerning the separation of church and state must be adjudicated on a case-by-case basis, it is also relevant that Alamo did not have the same history of interpersonal ties—such as those between Salvador Flores and Carmen Anaya—that preceded Palmer's formal engagement with Valley Interfaith as an Alliance School. Hence, the lack of bridging social capital may have played a greater role here than the presentation itself. But Alamo teachers still recognized that they needed help if they were to engage parents in their children's education.[5]

Elisabeth Valdez, another Valley Interfaith organizer, then tried a more exploratory and dialogic approach. She met with teachers and parents and discovered that in spite of the fact that the school enrolled roughly eight hundred students, meetings of the Parent-Teacher Organization usually were attended by no more than twenty parents. She stressed to the teachers that the idea of Alliance Schools was not to force change on reticent educators, but to develop positive relationships with the community that could make their work easier and more effective. Ramirez invited Salvador Flores to speak with his teachers about Palmer's work with Valley Interfaith, and Flores described the many benefits that he felt the collaboration had brought to his work with the community. Finally, Valdez invited Alamo teachers to attend statewide meetings of the Alliance Schools; at those meetings teachers learned that a whole network of schools working with community-based organizations was developing throughout Texas, and was doing so in a manner that stressed accountability and the building of broad networks of civic engagement. Within the Rio Grande Valley, Palmer had initiated the process, but schools in Brownsville, McAllen, and a number of the smaller cities between them were also coming on board. While most of the schools joining the network were elementary schools, Travis Middle School in McAllen had become the first secondary school in the Valley to become an Alliance School. Thanks to Valdez' tact, Ramirez' support, Flores' testimony, and the development of a supportive regional network, the idea of developing Alamo into an Alliance School became attractive once more to the teachers.

Working closely with Valdez, the middle school initiated "Alamo Community Walks" in September 1993. To help insure that the walks would be a success, Valdez drew upon the social capital embedded in religious institutions to prepare parents to receive the teachers well and to benefit from their conversations. "Community leaders from Resurrection Catholic Church helped us to prepare the parents," Alamo assistant principal David Cortez recalled, "and to break down the barriers between the school and the community, such as language barriers or the simple intimidation that parents felt when talking to a teacher." Twice a year teachers and parents left on a Saturday morning at eight o'clock and returned at noon after visiting the homes of students.[6]

The walks began effecting a sea change in the attitudes of teachers and parents toward one another. Teachers learned about the struggles that many parents experienced simply making ends meet, and parents learned that their teachers were genuinely concerned about their children. "Through our first walks the organizers helped us to see the community," one teacher observed. "We don't always see all of that in the school." To further consolidate the ties between the school and the community, René Ramirez and the teachers used the home visits to invite the parents to come to the school for an assembly. "Many parents are just waiting for us to invite them, to let them know that we need their ideas and support," he said. Each assembly was developed by Ramirez and his colleagues into an opportunity for the parents to acquaint themselves with community leaders—Alamo's mayor, or the superintendent of schools, or school board members—and to render transparent the internal operations of the school.[7]

One of the noteworthy features of the overall process of community involvement of the schools in the Pharr–San Juan–Alamo district entailed administrative leadership at the district level. Unlike the situation in many urban districts across the state, the superintendents in the Valley have by and large been supportive of the Alliance School strategy of parental engagement. This leadership was evident in the superintendent's comments to Ramirez encouraging the coalition with Valley Interfaith, and it has also been manifested in indispensable forms of technical support for the schools. At Alamo, for example, superintendents have authorized the use of school buses to transport low-income parents without their own transportation to Valley Interfaith accountability sessions pertaining to school board elections. At Palmer, superintendents have approved of Flores' use of money for substitutes so that teachers can visit parents' homes during the school day. Superintendents have also approved the use of school buses to transport parents to Alliance School meetings in Austin and Houston. Flores received the support of the school board—as well as that of his superintendent—for the use of Alliance School funds to send a teacher and a librarian to a two-week leadership training institute in Los Angeles provided by the IAF for community leaders. This district leadership—which is highly unusual among the Alliance Schools in Texas—has done a great deal to foster the high levels of trust and continuity between the schools and the community, and has reassured teachers that the development of new and innovative relationships with parents will be seen as an enhancement of education rather than a detraction from instruction.

Once the teachers' efforts began garnering increased parental engagement with Alamo Middle School, they agreed formally to become an Alliance School. One of the first and most palpable benefits of this decision was additional funding. Although the $15,000 that was provided in the first year of funding might not seem like much, for a school in a small and financially strapped district it enabled teachers to participate in valuable professional development workshops. "I was on the first group to draw up the proposal for funding with the Alliance Schools," teacher Allen Cox recalled, "and we had a lot of great ideas about funding English as a second language classes for parents, and computer training, and lots of stuff that would make sure that this school was fully used by the community." In addition, Alliance School meetings with guest speakers from leading research universities and smaller gatherings with principals from similar schools in low-income communities around the state enabled Ramirez and his colleagues to gain new ideas from others struggling with similar problems. Perhaps most important, however, was the larger cultural change entailed in shifting teachers' attention from curriculum and assessment to the broader identities and concerns of the students they taught. "As an Alliance School we focus on the whole student," Ramirez said, "not just the individual that happens to be within our walls. We look at the whole environment—the streets in our community, health issues, jobs, crime—and try to understand what this means for our students. And we know that there are changes that need to happen not only in our school but also in our community."[8]

Simultaneous with the initiation of the Alliance School partnership at Alamo, René Ramirez and his colleagues evaluated the development of the first teacher team in Alamo. There were many problems that first year. For one, each of the teachers on the team had inordinately large classes—Darvin Koenig remembered that they averaged thirty-six students. For another, because teachers on the team had time for a "team conference" in addition to their "personal conference," other teachers resented what they construed as an arbitrary perk. A further point of jealousy among many staff was that, other than Martinez, all of the teachers on the team were young and comparatively inexperienced; some veteran teachers felt that they had been unfairly passed over and would have gladly welcomed two conferences in their workday. In spite of the problems, however, the first teacher team reported enthusiastic results with its students, and other teachers and students were eager to give it a try also.

The transition to the team structure was not always easy for the teachers, who despite their desires for a more collaborative spirit often encountered difficulties in working with one another when it came to the intricacies of curriculum design and assessment. To ease this process, Ramirez created a new position in the school, that of a "facilitator" who would work in a nonjudgmental fashion with teams and with individuals to make sure that the middle school structure could succeed. He hired Oliver Nayola, a sixth grade science teacher who had previously taught at Farias Elementary School and had been at Alamo since its inception, to fill the position, and it became Nayoia's task to help the teachers develop their skills with conflict resolution, decision making, and the forming of consensus.

Nayola was a young teacher at the time, and many of his colleagues questioned his selection. Given those reservations, he had to demonstrate a high level of devotion to his colleagues. "We worked hard to help the teams to see each other as part of a family," he said. "In a family, we care for each other, and we help each other. If you're having problems, I don't turn my back on you." Nayola visited the classes of teachers, and while he made suggestions for areas of improvement, he was not formally evaluating them on an "instrument" designed by the Texas Education Agency or another tool that would affect their careers and salaries. As a result, teachers saw his visits as a form of genuine support, and the transition to the new teams gradually began to win over reluctant teachers or those who had difficulties with the structural reorganization of the school.[9]

In the ensuing years Alamo developed ten teams of teachers, and teachers and students worked together to find creative names for their learning communities; some of the finalists were the "Starcatchers," the "Killer Bees," the "Determinators," the "Dream Team," the "Challengers," the "Texas Tornadoes," and the "Rainbow Riders." It is intriguing to observe how local culture informed the selection of the names: the "Texas Tornadoes" is a Tejano band that plays a lively blend of polka melodies and rock rhythms indigenous to Mexican Americans in South Texas; the "Challengers" is a reference to the failed space mission that exploded over the NASA base in Clear Lake, Texas, in 1986. To strengthen a sense of group identity that is so important for middle school students, teacher and student teams have developed logos, their own T-shirts, and even their own stationery with team letterhead. In addition, they have developed a lively sense of competition that is translated into athletic events, school festivals, and friendly banter with one another. "That change was the best thing that ever happened in our school," Ramirez enthused, and noted with pride that the three other middle schools in his district all followed Alamo's lead in this regard in subsequent years.[10]

Teachers credit the new team structure with enhancing their control of the curriculum and scheduling. They have designed multiple interdisciplinary projects that weave together community concerns with academic curricula. One teacher team developed a major thematic unit on the weather in which students learned about the causes of flooding in the Valley and in their colonias. Others have studied the family, the ocean, or Native Americans, in each instance making use of local resources to provide depth and texture to the units. As a result of the interdisciplinary collaboration, teachers can help each other with students' academic skills across the curriculum. "I teach math, but I make sure that my kids write also because that's important for the TAAS," one teacher said, "and I always compare notes with my team on how the kids are doing so that we can identify areas of weakness together and think about how we can help the kids to overcome them. And because I know what the other teachers are doing, I can talk about how the same kinds of inference and analysis that you might use in an English or a science classroom can be used in math. I don't know if I'd be doing any of this if my only contacts outside of class were with a math department."

Teachers have also found the team structure to help with maintaining classroom discipline. "In my first year teaching here, I had a hard time keeping control of my classes," one young teacher commented, "and there was one girl who got angry and kicked me in the shin. And I don't know what I would have done if I didn't have my team to turn to, and we hadn't forced her to sit down with all of us to talk about her attitude and things she could do to improve her schoolwork." In addition, teachers report that they experience a far greater impact with parents when discussing discipline issues if they conduct such conversations as a group so that parents understand that misconduct is not restricted to one particular teacher.

Simultaneous with the development of greater personalization and interdisciplinary curricular units, René Ramirez also worked to improve the visual beauty of Alamo. He commissioned a local artist to paint murals in the school to inspire students to excel and celebrate local culture through the portrayal of traditional Mexican dances. It is indicative of the sense of ownership and pride in the school that the murals have stood intact for years with no vandalism marring the color and profile they lend to the school's hallways.

It was not long after the implementation of all these changes prompted by the new team structure, however, that the school board of the Pharr–San Juan–Alamo district almost upset the continuity in personal relationships that is at the core of Alamo's middle school concept. A new elementary school, North Alamo, had been built nearby, and the school board and superintendent wanted to remove the sixth graders from the middle school and place them in it. But Ramirez and his teachers didn't want to surrender the sense of community that takes time to mature in a school and that they felt was better provided by three years of stability in a school rather than two. "Basically, the teachers organized the parents," Valley Interfaith organizer Elizabeth Valdez said, "and once the parents understood what was at stake, they educated the rest of the parents." Those parents held a series of house meetings with friends and neighbors to discuss their concerns; they also met at Resurrection Catholic Church to gauge the community's feelings about the proposed change. Finally, parents organized meetings with individual school board members—called "one-on-one's" in IAF nomenclature—and told them that they liked the school culture that Alamo had developed and felt that it was truly helping the education of their children.[11]

The meetings between parents and school board members around the sixth grade at the middle school were not easy. School board members in the Pharr–San Juan–Alamo Independent School District were not accustomed to vocal parents speaking up about the reallocation of children from one school to another, and they expressed resentment at the challenges organized parents represented to their power. "I almost lost my job in that battle," René Ramirez said, "and I was told by a school board member that I had lost control of my school and that the parents had taken over." Elizabeth Valdez was impressed with Ramirez' leadership at this critical juncture. "He listened very carefully to what the parents and staff wanted to do," she said, "and he helped to create a culture where the parents could take some ownership of the school." In spite of the political risks entailed, the community fought the proposed change. Teachers such as Diane Hinojosa presented their objections before the school board, and in a new show of the power that a united community can yield, persuaded the board to vote unanimously to allow the sixth grade to remain at Alamo. It was a turning point for René Ramirez, the teachers, and the parents. "It was only then that we realized that our school had really changed," he recalled, "and that we really had the parents behind us."[12]

Rather than use the community support as an excuse for complacency, the staff at Alamo continued to look for new strategies to improve their school. Throughout the 1994-95 school year Ramirez questioned the faculty about ideas that could help the children, and became increasingly intrigued by "block scheduling." This form of scheduling allows teachers to have more time to teach in-depth units—typically, ninety-minute "blocks"—than is possible in the usual fifty-minute class periods. With the consent of the teachers, parents, and students, the path was laid to begin block scheduling in the 1995-96 school year.

In the summer of 1995, Ramirez was appointed to become the principal of Pharr–San Juan–Alamo High School. He was replaced by Rosi Ruiz, who had been an assistant principal at the school since its inception. Like Salvador Flores, Carmen Anaya, and many other civic leaders in the Valley, Ruiz is an immigrant; she was born in the small village of Hualahaises in Nuevo León and moved to the United States with her parents when she was one year old. She attended Palmer (when it was named Edison) and the public schools in Pharr and Alamo, and graduated from PSJA in 1970. Like the majority of the population of her generation in the Valley, she grew up closely linked to agriculture, not through planting, tending, or harvesting crops, but by packing tomatoes, beets, and okra in Alamo's major packing center, Alamo Produce. She graduated from Pan American University in three years, majoring in Spanish, and was always motivated to help Mexican Americans to retain and improve their Spanish. She returned to PSJA as a teacher in 1973 and taught English and Spanish there for fourteen years. Then followed a one-year break to work for the district, coordinating language arts instruction at the middle school level; she visited three campuses to monitor and improve the instruction of English teachers. She then was hired as an assistant principal at the brand-new Alamo Middle School, which opened in the fall of 1988.

Rosi Ruiz inherited a school that had developed momentum under the leadership of René Ramirez, but she was determined to place her own imprint on the building. Two of the major reforms that have occurred under her leadership are the completion of the transition to block scheduling and the implementation of a process of peer mediation in which students learn how to intervene and resolve conflicts between themselves. The transition to block scheduling has seen relatively minor disruptions in the school. In most of the teams, teachers use a form of block scheduling in which different classes are held on Tuesdays and Thursdays than on Mondays, Wednesdays, and Fridays. Yet it is intriguing to note that teams have abundant freedom to experiment with their own structures and that the collaborative structure seems to enhance teacher autonomy rather than constrain it. The Starcatcher team, for example, uses an accelerated form of block scheduling in which team members teach the same students every day for three weeks; they then rotate the classes. In addition, the Starcatchers decided that they wanted to keep the same students for two years in a row, which team members enjoy because of their ability to trace students' progress over a longer period of time. Somewhat like a federal system in which states are interdependent in some areas and autonomous in others, Alamo has developed a culture in which teams of teachers can develop their own professional judgment about the best way to educate their pupils.

The ramifications of teacher autonomy in the classroom appear to be felicitous for teachers and students alike. Diane Hinojosa, an eighth grade English teacher, can expose her students to challenging texts such as Ecclesiastes for a unit on the Bible as literature; others, such as Darvin Koenig, select books such as Judith Ortiz Cofer's *An Island like You*, which consists of a series of rich vignettes about the beauty and the challenges of growing up in a low-income Hispanic community. Throughout the school, there is an easy intermingling of Spanish and English in classroom conversation, with teachers proficient enough in Spanish to respond to student banter in an informal, relaxed manner.

Peer mediation is another transformation that has had a major impact upon Alamo's culture. The students who have been trained in mediation have placed posters throughout the school urging their peers to use them as resources, and they all have been used to consult with their peers repeatedly. In one particularly bold move, a seventh grade girl—

herself a peer mediator—asked another mediator to help her resolve a conflict with a teacher. The mediation was successful, and the student now understands the basis for their misunderstanding and comments that the teacher "is a cool guy."

In spite of the many new programs and experiments, Alamo still has abundant issues with which its faculty struggle. Although the gangs that dominated the campus in its first few years have disappeared—at least in terms of their visibility on campus—security and discipline issues are still salient. "Don't get me wrong, because we still have problems with one or two kids in the school," Oliver Nayola confided. "But it's nothing compared to what we had before." Once or twice a year, a small cluster of students will try out a gang initiation rite called "la bamba" on a willing victim in a bathroom; it is nothing less than a mass assault on the individual, which usually is detected before too much trouble is done. In the spring of 1999 a student brought a gun to school, and while it was confiscated by campus security officers without anyone being injured, the incident highlighted the need for continued vigilance about safety at the school. In addition, Alamo's in-school suspension system for students with discipline problems seemed to be viewed by repeat offenders as something of a joke or even a blessing in disguise, since it essentially gave students time out of classes they were otherwise required to attend; in addition, they regularly were the first students served lunch in the cafeteria. While no easy solution appeared to be immediately available, the faculty began a search for alternative forms of discipline that would be viewed by students as more serious in their outcomes.[13]

As for Valley Interfaith, its presence at Alamo has continued to be contested throughout the history of the collaboration. The first presentation by Valley Interfaith at Alamo provoked much anxiety and resistance among teachers to the idea of a collaboration with the community organization, and although Elizabeth Valdez was able to repair that, subsequent difficulties have ensued. Industrial Areas Foundation organizers, in line with their principle of the "iron rule"—the notion that one should never do for others what they are capable of doing for themselves—often move on to another site quickly after organizing one school. This was indeed the case at Alamo, where unlike the situation at Palmer, the principal was not herself a Valley Interfaith leader. After mentoring Alamo faculty in effective strategies for home visits, organizer Elisabeth Valdez exited the campus altogether.

The diminished presence of Valley Interfaith on the Alamo campus produced grumbling among teachers there in the following years, and points to a particular tension that accompanies the actualization of the iron rule. For while some educators are pleased to know that IAF organizations plan to teach a new kind of community engagement and then to depart, respecting the capacity of educators to develop social capital as best they see fit, other teachers seek a more sustained relationship and guidance. "When I voted to partner with Valley Interfaith, I thought that I was voting for them to really be here on campus to help us to organize our relationships with the community better," one teacher complained. "Instead, they only seem to show up when they have a meeting coming up and want our participation." Teachers on one team felt clearly manipulated when they were asked by an assistant principal at Alamo to support Valley Interfaith's "sign up and take charge" campaign of voter registration in September 1997. "This really isn't part of our job," one seasoned veteran complained, "and I don't see why we should get out and support Valley Interfaith's agenda when we haven't seen hide nor hair of them for a long time now."

Teachers' resistance to Valley Interfaith reveals a point of friction where professional autonomy and community engagement are not easily combined. On the one hand, when teachers perceive a lack of evidence of support by Valley Interfaith for their school, this interpretation can aptly be criticized as a kind of selective perception, for teachers would likely be upset to lose the programs that Alliance School funds support, such as peer mediation, parent education classes, and professional development for teachers. On the other hand, the teachers' resentment in this particular case stemmed from a sense that Valley Interfaith was encroaching on their professional autonomy. The fact that an assistant principal asked the teachers to support Valley Interfaith's agenda may also be seen as reflective of a schism between administration and faculty who are reluctant to follow the administration's politics, even if Valley Interfaith claims to be nonpartisan.

It was not until two months later, in November 1997, that Valley Interfaith organizer Estela Sosa-Garza attended a faculty meeting at Alamo. At that time she sought to elicit faculty support for an evening event that would welcome parents into the school and ask them in small group settings what they like or do not like about Alamo. As one might anticipate given the context, some teachers vocally expressed skepticism. One teacher was concerned that the meetings would be "superficial" and would fail to impress upon the parents just how weak their children's academic work was and the need for full parental support in the effort to bring their children's work up to grade level. "I don't think we need to ask parents what they like or don't like about our school, like Valley Interfaith says," he commented, "I think we need to let the parents know that their kids are achieving at a level far lower than what they're capable of. We need to give the parents a wake-up call." He was supported by a colleague, who remarked, "I grew up in the colonias in San Juan and I know what the conditions there are. I don't need to hear about that. But the minute our kids get home, the parents speak to them only in Spanish, they watch Univision, and everything that we're trying to do here gets washed away. We take one step forward here, and the kids go home, and it's two steps back. We need to tell the parents that they need to be much more active to help their kids to succeed or the whole cycle is just going to be perpetuated all over again."

It was an auspicious moment for Alamo, where the principles of the Alliance School network met head-on with the wariness of hard-working veteran teachers. Yet it is important to note that no teachers spoke out against increased communication between the school and the parents; rather, the *nature* of that communication was questioned. Valley Interfaith, sensitive to the intimidation that many low-income parents feel when entering a school, sought to win the parents' trust and to engage their critical thinking by creating a forum in which parents would feel that the school genuinely cared about their perceptions and sentiments. Oppositional teachers, on the other hand, felt it imperative that the school impress upon the parents both the need to reorient everyday household cultural patterns to promote greater academic success and the need to be forthright about students' level of academic ability.

It should be noted that the oppositional teachers' positions should not be interpreted as either conservative or assimilationist. One of the teachers is a lifelong labor activist who has taught citizenship classes at the headquarters of the United Farmworkers union in Texas. Another strongly believes in the importance of multilingual abilities and speaks not only Spanish and English but also two Filipino dialects that he has acquired from his Filipino wife and her extended family. Rather, the issue has much more to do with the precise kinds of strategies that Alamo Middle School should adopt as part of its parent-engagement program, and with the wager that the dialogic approach that Valley Interfaith uses may not be as productive as the adaptation of more didactic strategies to promote students' academic success.

When encountering teacher resistance of this nature, principals are placed in a difficult position. If they endorse uncritically teachers' opposition, they may unwittingly support the interpretation of parents as culprits, which could undermine strong school-community ties. On the other hand, if they simply defend the plans of community organizations, they are likely to be seen by veteran teachers not only as naive but also as disloyal to the faculty. In this case, Rosi Ruiz was outspoken in her support of Valley Interfaith, while simultaneously allowing teachers to express their reservations with both passion and eloquence. Reviewing all of the positive changes that have occurred at Alamo over the previous seven years, Ruiz told her faculty, "This is the way we've always operated. We try something out, there is some resistance at the start, but we give it our best shot, iron out the kinks, and then it becomes a part of us. I've heard a lot of you say that we need to get the parents more involved. Here is our opportunity." With that prudent approach, teachers agreed to give the idea of the parent meetings at the school a chance.

When the parent meetings did convene at Alamo in early December 1997, the turnout began slowly on a Monday night meeting for sixth graders but gained momentum on a Tuesday night meeting for seventh graders and especially on a Thursday night meeting for the parents of eighth grade students. Some teacher teams prepared supper for the parents as a sign of hospitality. "Some of the parents had real hard-core concerns," assistant principal David Cortez recalled afterward. "They really got down to the nitty-gritty about issues facing their children, and a couple got pretty nasty. One in particular wanted more individual attention for her child, so I met with her the following day, and we really got into it. But I see it as real progress, because we need to air out our differences, and they need to know that we want to put in the time to meet their needs."[14]

The parent meetings were viewed in a variety of ways by Alamo faculty. Some felt that the parent turnout indicated that parents were anything but apathetic about their children's academic achievement. It is true that not many parents came to the first (Monday evening) meeting, but once the word got out to the community that the teachers were truly listening to the parents, turnout increased in the latter part of the week. "In fact, we were told by many parents that we need more meetings like these," Cortez said, "and I think we were all pleased that there were so many good discussions, and that we recognized that we all really want to do what is best for the kids."[15]

On the other hand, some teachers were skeptical. "Look, we can get the parents to turn out if we serve them dinner," one teacher said.

"But if we don't prepare something real concrete like food to get them to our meetings, they don't show up. For me, what I've seen doesn't count as real parental involvement."

When one turns to TAAS data for Alamo students, the results indicate steady improvement over the years. For the full data on Alamo, consult the appendix. In 1994 Alamo students were struggling with the TAAS. Sixth graders performed worse than their peers at the district and the state level, and disadvantaged Alamo sixth graders performed worse than their peers at the state level. At the seventh grade level, Alamo students outperformed their peers in the district, but not the state, and there was little difference between disadvantaged students and their peers at the state level in reading and mathematics. Eighth graders likewise outperformed the district, and lagged behind the state; however, disadvantaged students performed worse than their peers at the state level. Eighth grade writing scores exhibit that the general pattern suggested above continues: Alamo students performed better than the district and worse than the state. In this instance, however, disadvantaged Alamo students outperformed their peers at the state level. This achievement should be relativized, however, since more than a third of those students failed to pass the writing section.

From these inauspicious beginnings Alamo's TAAS results have shown a pattern of steady improvement in subsequent years. The rate of improvement of sixth grade students in reading and math from 1993 to 1999 surpasses that of both the state and the district. If present trends continue, Alamo will overtake the state and district passing percentages in the next few years. In a particularly striking achievement, disadvantaged sixth graders at Alamo climbed from a low of 39 percent passing on the math test in 1994 to surpass the state passing rate of 86 percent in 1999.

Gains in seventh grade reading scores at Alamo have been modest, as have been the gains at the state and district level, but once again the mathematics gains have been dramatic (almost 30% from 1994 to 1999). Eighth grade reading scores have improved steadily, and we can extrapolate that the school will surpass the state if present trends continue. Mathematics gains have also been strong for eighth graders; Alamo students outperform not only district students but also Texas students, with disadvantaged students at Alamo outperforming disadvantaged students across the state by a wide margin. Alamo eighth graders now outperform at the state and district levels on the writing section of the TAAS as well.

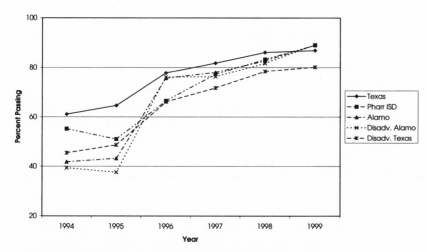

Grade 6 TAAS Math Test, Alamo Middle School, 1994–1999.

Alamo would thus appear to be on a strong upward trajectory in terms of academic achievement at the sixth and eighth grade levels, with slower increases for seventh graders. Many faculty are pleased with their students' achievement on the test. However, it is also important to note that many are angry about the emphasis on the TAAS in the school and frustrated by their students' continued difficulties on the test. "We have to remember that the TAAS is a *minimum* skills test," one teacher commented, "and we're still not excelling even on that measure." Other teachers worry that so much attention is focused on the TAAS in the school that students' higher-level, critical thinking skills are rarely engaged. "If I just taught to the test, I'd completely lose my kids," one English teacher commented, "and besides, it wouldn't even be right. How are you ever going to get a love of literature or develop any complexity in your thinking by cramming for the TAAS?"

While one should appreciate Alamo's gains in student achievement on the TAAS, one should also recognize the costs paid by teachers and students to reap those results. The chair of the school's language arts program, Diane Hinojosa, took twelve-minute lunch breaks from August through January of the 1998-99 school year so that she could intensely tutor more than fifty students over the lunch period to boost their TAAS writing scores. When the results came in, 95 percent of her students had passed. She cried and so did many of her students and colleagues. "They really weren't sure that they could do it," she recalled, "and when the results came in it was such a victory for them." The poignant part of this story is that teachers and students deserve lunch breaks, and while it is gratifying to know that the students passed, the manner in which standardized tests are driving teachers and students to abandon hitherto sacrosanct times to catch one's breath and reflect on the morning's events raises concerns.[16]

By the fall of 1999 the major issue on the campus was neither academic achievement nor community engagement, but a new school discipline program that had been developed by a team of students, teachers, and parents convening together over many months. The new plan called for the inculcation of military-type discipline on campus for repeat offenders. Students who threatened other students, continuously disrupted instruction, or scrawled graffiti on bathroom walls would go through a three-stage process that began with warnings and escalated to a bootcamp program in which two faculty dressed in army boots and camouflaged uniforms would supervise students in cleaning up the campus and learning military discipline.[17]

On many campuses the proposal of such a program would provoke a firestorm of controversy. During a site visit in August 1999, however, I observed little opposition from students, parents, and faculty. On the contrary, the tone on campus seemed to be relief that a program with serious sanctions was finally in place. "I simply will not tolerate it that a child who comes to our campus to learn is bullied in the bathroom, or is even afraid to go to the bathroom because of kids he might encounter there," one teacher remarked. "For a lot of these kids our schools are the only way that they're going to get out of their colonias, and for us to send the message that our school isn't worth maintaining as a safe and orderly environment is unconscionable." Even some of the most outspoken critics of the school administration agreed to give the new discipline program a chance. "Everybody had a say in developing this new strategy," one teacher said, "and I think we have to send a clear message in this area. This is one way to do it."

Teachers' enthusiasm for the new discipline plan developed entirely separate from any kind of relationship with Valley Interfaith and reflected just how far the school's staff had moved away from its ties to the community organization. By the fall of 1999 the collaboration between Alamo Middle School and Valley Interfaith was in trouble. The small group of faculty who truly believed in the importance of community engagement were exhausted by the constant rounds of meetings that were called by Valley Interfaith that they felt bore meager results. "I've got two kids at home," one teacher complained, "and it's not right for me to be coming home at nine o'clock, long after they've gone to bed, or to be out at workshops all day on Saturdays." Another teacher commented, "As far as I can tell, the Alliance has fizzled out. It was good when we were first getting started, because it really did get us together with the parents and the community. But now we're in a different place. We've internalized all of that and need to move on."

In private conversations, other teachers expressed a number of complaints about Valley Interfaith. "How come the organizers so often seem to be White?" one Mexican American teacher wondered. "What does that say about us that we seem to need White folks to come in from outside of the Valley to organize us? I grew up in Las Milpas. I know what our needs are." Others felt that the claim of the community-based organization to be interdenominational was fraudulent. "Are there any Protestant churches in Valley Interfaith?" one teacher asked. "As far as I can tell, the folks in charge seem to be pretty much one nun after another."

Valley Interfaith had defenders on campus. "They always bring out all of their congregations when there's a school board meeting and the issue is raising teacher salaries," said one teacher, "and you have to appreciate that." "Is it Valley Interfaith's fault if we don't have our troops organized to support their programs?" another teacher questioned. "If we're honest about it, the issues that they work on like colonias and job training directly benefit our community. I'm not hearing much from my colleagues about how we as educators need to demonstrate commitment to this community as part of this partnership."

Others rejected the claim that Valley Interfaith was dominated by Whites. "Ernie Cortés, Elizabeth Valdez, Estela Sosa-Garza—do they look White to you?" one veteran teacher asked. Finally, regarding the claim that Valley Interfaith really is not interdenominational, one teacher said, "Look, it's true that as far as we can tell, it really is a Catholic organization. But look at where we are. The Valley is just about 100 percent Catholic."

However persuasive these rejoinders from the defenders of Valley Interfaith may be, they did not seem to hold much weight with the majority of Alamo teachers in the fall of 1999. The major lure that the Alliance Schools offered that the teachers appreciated at that time were the potential funds—$45,000 over two years—that would enable them to attend professional development conferences. Yet even those did not appear sacrosanct. "We go up to Houston or Austin and see some truly dynamite presentations by other schools that really seem to be on the move," a teacher said. "I was especially impressed by the presentation by a Black school in the north of Houston. But then we get on the plane and fly back here and go straight back to doing things the way we've always done them. I'm not seeing follow-through." Reflecting the troubled nature of the relationship with Valley Interfaith, Alamo faculty voted against even applying for a renewal of Alliance School funds in November 1999.

For Rosi Ruiz, the faculty ambivalence about Valley Interfaith was problematic. "I can tell them that this is good for our school, and many of them will be in favor of continuing the relationship just because of that," she said. "But that doesn't help us if we're not going to really be committed to working together." Alamo's faculty had been skeptical of the collaboration with Valley Interfaith from the very beginning of the relationship in the fall of 1993, and time did not appear to have strengthened the affiliation. The hidden costs of social capitalization—in terms of teachers' additional workload, distraction from an academic focus, and uncertainty of results—had taken a toll on all parties.[18]

CHAPTER FOUR

TRANSFORMING SAM HOUSTON ELEMENTARY SCHOOL

In the early 1990s Sam Houston Elementary School could be found in the heart of a barrio called La Paloma by its inhabitants in south-central McAllen, Texas. Although McAllen is a small city by most measures, Sam Houston's immediate environment appeared very similar to the West Side of San Antonio or the East Side of Austin; tiny shacks packed with immigrant families alternated with more stable middle-class homes, and all kinds of farm animals, ranging from roosters to goats, could be seen in small backyards or wandering into the streets, indicating just how close ostensibly urban residents remained to the pace and texture of rural life. Sam Houston served a low-income Mexican American community that witnessed scant evidence of the growing prosperity of McAllen's North Side. First opened in 1920, Sam Houston was the oldest public school in McAllen. Regretfully, the district had allowed the building to run down, and it was badly in need of structural repairs.

Sam Houston's principal was Connie Maheshwari. The daughter of Carmen and José Anaya, Maheshwari had traveled with her parents as a migrant laborer throughout the 1960s and 1970s and had lived out her parents' dream that she acquire an education and enter a profession. Once she had graduated from Pan American University in nearby Edinburg and entered teaching, Maheshwari observed her mother's political development with Valley Interfaith around the issue of colonias improvement in Las Milpas. Maheshwari harbors no hard feelings about the poverty that confronted her when she grew up: "My mother taught us to be strong and persistent, and my father taught us to be open and accepting. When you have parents like that, you might not have much money, but you're so rich that it's really unbelievable."[1]

Maheshwari entered teaching in 1979 at Wilson Elementary School and was the assistant principal at Rayburn Elementary School in McAllen from 1987 to 1990. She was appointed principal of Sam Houston in the fall of 1990 and spent several years developing her leadership skills and struggling to improve the academic achievements of the more than five hundred children in attendance. She first became interested in the Alliance School partnership with Valley Interfaith when Father Bart Flaat of Saint Joseph's the Worker Catholic Church in South McAllen set up a meeting to promote the new school network in McAllen in January 1994.

Father Bart's leadership of the Alliance School initiative in South McAllen provides a marked point of contrast to the situation at Palmer and Alamo, where clergy have played a less visible role in the development of the school reform effort. Saint Joseph's provides a dramatic exemplification of the notion that strong and active church leadership can play a powerful role in developing the civic capacities of low-income citizens and immigrants.[2]

Father Bart had been active with Communities Organized for Public Services (COPS) in San Antonio from 1977 to 1985, where he was recruited into the community-based organization by Robert Rivera, the lead organizer at that time. When Father Bart accepted a position at Our Lady of the Assumption in Harlingen in 1985, he attempted to join Valley Interfaith immediately, but instead had to spend two years working with his parishioners to develop their trust in the organization before they agreed to become dues-paying members. Yet even when they did join, the cautious congregation never developed the civic leadership of which Father Bart was persuaded they were capable.

Father Bart discovered a similar atmosphere at Saint Joseph's when he took over its leadership in 1991. Although Saint Joseph's supported Valley Interfaith, Father Bart considered it to be a "sleeping member," one that rarely organized in any active way to support the agenda of the community-based organization. Yet Father Bart sensed a hunger for change among many individuals with whom he had his first contacts in his parish, which comprises a number of neighborhoods—La Paloma, Hermosa, Balboa, Alta Linda, and Los Encinos—in South McAllen. To ascertain the depth of such sentiments, Father Bart began a series of conversations in the community. "We held thirty house meetings in my first two months in McAllen," he said, "and I met over two thousand people who live here. And basically, I asked them to tell me two things: first, their stories, and second, their dreams. I wanted to know what they hoped for, what they dreamed for. And once they had told me that, I had a pretty good agenda."[3]

For Father Bart, the issues that confronted his parishioners were twofold and resulted in a parish development program that he established with the most active church leaders. "First, we wanted a clinic for people who fell between the cracks—who had neither Medicaid nor health insurance—and we learned that there were loads of people like this in South McAllen. Second, we heard a lot about schools and education. A lot of our parents have very little education, and schools are very intimidating institutions for them. And our parents wanted to get involved, but they wanted to do more than just folding papers at the school."[4]

Saint Joseph's the Worker became a lively religious community in the months following Father Bart's arrival. He established thirty *comunidades de base* in his parish, where laity met on a weekly basis, discussed troubles in their neighborhood, and explored passages from scripture to explicate their relevance to their challenges. They discussed crime, unemployment, and family problems, and Father Bart worked with his leading parishioners to interpret their concerns in light of Catholic theology. "Whenever you see people who are oppressed because of an economic system, our scripture gives us a very clear message that we need to empower people, to help them make sense of their lives, and to help them to gain the power to make decisions and to reach out in new kinds of ways," he commented. Father Bart attempted to model a particularly energetic kind of church leadership to their parish by following up their group discussions with individual meetings and visits. He sought to ensure that the parishioners' needs were addressed and to be an advocate for them whenever possible.[5]

The heightened engagement with Catholic theology in the parish of Saint Joseph's resulted in concrete forms of political action. Parishioners educated themselves on the importance of voting and supported voter registration drives organized by Valley Interfaith in South Mc-Allen. They agitated for improved health care, and collaborated with the city council to create a clinic called El Milagro to meet the needs of low-income citizens and immigrants who otherwise could not access affordable medical care. Many parishioners were alarmed by increasingly brazen acts of crime in their neighborhoods—one incident had led to the deaths of two youths and a police officer in the summer of 1993. As a result, they began a series of meetings with the police to enhance security. Concerning the community's desire for improved education, Father

Bart was intrigued to learn of the creation of the Alliance Schools in the summer of 1992, and for the following year he promoted the new network in his discussions with public school principals in South McAllen. Another round of roughly fifty house meetings was convened throughout La Paloma at the same time—using the *comunidades de base* as the forum for announcing and organizing the meetings—to discuss the emerging political agenda for the community.

All of these different organizing initiatives came together in a "Parish Convention" held at Saint Joseph's in September 1993, attended by more than six hundred parishioners and community residents, where a host of different issues, engendered through months of individual conversations and house meetings, coalesced into a coherent program of neighborhood development to promote the well-being of the families living on the South Side. Parishioners had invited several public officials, such as school board members, city council members, and the chief of police, and they received commitments from the officials to help them with problems such as unpaved roads, drive-by shootings, and disrepair of school buildings.

These diverse efforts resulted in more than two thousand signatures on a petition supporting Valley Interfaith's agenda. School board members, however, seemed to be particularly opposed to any kind of long-term collaboration between public schools and Valley Interfaith. Under the influence of Mayor Othal Brand, an outspoken critic of Valley Interfaith, many public officials had developed a hands-off approach to the community-based organization. Fortunately for the Alliance School effort, however, the McAllen superintendent of schools, Dr. José Lopez, had had positive experiences with COPS in San Antonio, and he played a key role in persuading school board members to meet with Valley Interfaith organizers and leaders. Father Bart Flaat and Sister Maria Sánchez of Saint Joseph's met with each school board member and all of the principals in the schools in south-central McAllen to discuss the potential of the Alliance School network to educate parents to become better advocates for their children. When the Texas Industrial Areas Foundation organized a large conference for prospective Alliance Schools in Houston in January 1994, six of the eight public schools in South McAllen attended.

The next step was a meeting set up by Flaat and Lopez to convene all of the public school principals in McAllen to discuss in greater detail the possibilities and risks that could attend becoming an Alliance School. At the meeting, some principals expressed concern that collaboration with Valley Interfaith could be interpreted by families as mixing politics—and radical politics at that—with the public schools. Others were worried about collaborating with the churches that provide the dues-paying backbone of Valley Interfaith, and raised issues about the separation of church and state. For several, however, the possibilities seemed to outweigh the risks. Connie Maheshwari was one of the principals invited to the meeting, and because of her mother's work with Valley Interfaith, she instantly was interested in the collaborative. "Connie was a strategic person for us in starting the Alliance Schools in McAllen," Sister Maria recalled, "because her mother was one of the first and strongest Valley Interfaith leaders who really got the organization going through her work on the colonias in Las Milpas. We knew that she was a person who would understand the kind of involvement with the community that we wanted to have."[6]

When Maheshwari returned to her campus after the meeting convened by Flaat and Lopez and began discussing the idea of the Alliance Schools with her staff, she found that some teachers shared some of the concerns raised by principals at the meeting. Teachers were particularly concerned that collaboration with the Alliance Schools network could entail a loss of their sense of professional autonomy. "Teachers are afraid that Valley Interfaith is going to come in and tell them what to do," Maheshwari recalled. "This is a real fear." She also noted that several teachers were worried that empowered parents "could become a monster" who might at first conduct purposeful advocacy for their children but then develop an adversarial tone with teachers. It took her several months to work patiently with her staff to persuade them that the Alliance School concept represented a calculated risk that could benefit their students by improving relationships between their homes and the school.[7]

Sam Houston became the first Alliance School in McAllen and formally joined the Alliance School network in April 1994. Unfortunately, the momentum developed on campus slowed when José Lopez, the supportive superintendent of schools, became involved in a scandal about his private affairs. He lost his job, the Alliance Schools in McAllen lost an important ally, and the school board began a search for a new superintendent.

Troubles at the top of the district enhanced the risks entailed in initiating a community-organizing approach to school reform in La Paloma, but they did not impede it. Once Sam Houston became an Alliance School, Valley Interfaith organizers began working closely with faculty and parents to develop leadership in the community. Mentored by Sister Pearl Ceasar and Estela Sosa-Garza of Valley Interfaith, teachers and staff at Sam Houston began learning the nuts-and-bolts of organizing in the summer and fall of 1994. They learned how to conduct "one-on-one's" and to quickly but respectfully identify individuals' issues. They learned how to do "power analyses" of the community that helped them to understand issues of accountability and control. Finally, they learned how to conduct "research actions" with public officials to identify latent resources, such as money or manpower, that could be used to attack the problems confronting their community.

Throughout the fall and winter of 1994 Valley Interfaith organizers, Sam Houston teachers, and indigenous community residents conducted scores of house meetings in the neighborhood surrounding Sam Houston. A host of issues were brought to the table. Parents complained about poor lighting and lack of supervision in the numerous back alleys that students took to and from school. Others worried about abandoned houses where teenagers met to sell and use drugs in close proximity to Sam Houston. Many parents, and especially single mothers, were concerned that they had to work full-time and had no way to supervise their children in the late afternoon. Other parents were simply worried about the abundance of trash—old tires, broken glass, rain-soaked mattresses —that littered the streets and alleys around the school and seemed to escape the attention of city sanitation workers. Finally, teachers from Sam Houston who attended the house meetings and those parents who were active in the school shared their concerns about the crumbling physical infrastructure of the school, the persistent presence of rats in classrooms and the cafeteria, and their hope for a new building.

"I loved those house meetings," Connie Maheshwari recalled, "because that's where I really learned about our community, and that's where our teachers began learning about the condition of children in our community. That's where we really started putting together a genuine curriculum unit that would enable us to become a true community of learners." Teachers were happy when parents who had been reluctant to come to the school approached them at house meetings, asked about ways that they could support their children's learning, and began coaching their children at home in ways that had real benefits for the children's academic achievement.[8]

Working closely with Valley Interfaith, the teachers and parents at Sam Houston established task forces to research and address each of the issues presented above. Valley Interfaith organizers taught the parents that if they wanted an after-school program they might be able to acquire the needed funds from McAllen's Department of Parks and Recreation. They helped the parents to understand that if they wanted greater security in their neighborhood, it was important to initiate a relationship with the police and to work together to target high-crime areas. With each of the different areas of concern, Valley Interfaith organizers helped the parents and the teachers to comprehend that they could develop the political clout to redirect city and school district revenues to improve their school and its community. And in each case, Valley Interfaith organizers and leaders worked with the parents and teachers to set up and lead meetings with the chief of police, school board members, city council members, and the director of McAllen's Department of Parks and Recreation.

One of the important developmental processes that happened through all of these actions is that parents and teachers were working together to improve educational conditions for Sam Houston's children, and they began to appreciate the talents that each group brought to the process. "I remember going with the parents to meet with the chief of police, Alex Longoria," Maheshwari said. "But I didn't lead the meeting. I simply listened to what the parents were saying. They did all of the talking, and they're the ones who had some real ideas for change worked out in advance. And once you've been through several meetings like that, you start to change and to understand that parents have strengths that somehow you never really saw or understood before."[9]

Not all of the house meetings were easy for Maheshwari and the teachers. Some parents vented pent-up frustrations with the school and the lack of infrastructure in the community in a way that blamed the educators. There were many times when Maheshwari and the teachers felt scapegoated and misunderstood. They persevered through these trials, however, hoping that the Valley Interfaith organizers who were guiding their work truly knew what they were doing during this critical juncture.

All of the "one-on-one's," house meetings, and task force undertakings reached a crescendo in January 1995, when the community worked with Valley Interfaith to prepare a large public assembly—which they called a "Kids' Action Assembly"—to create a greater climate of community accountability for the children. Estela Sosa-Garza of Valley Interfaith worked closely with parents and teachers, role-playing the statements that they wanted to make and the questions they wished to address to public officials. According to IAF community-organizing traditions, even if one has prior agreements from public officials to work together, it is crucial that those agreements take on a public texture before low-income communities. Those large assemblies mirror back to the community progress that has been made through many months of political organizing, and they also demonstrate the leadership that has been developed by indigenous community residents.

During this same period, Connie Maheshwari received phone calls from friends in city government who warned her that the parents' increasing activism and affiliation with Valley Interfaith was garnering her enemies among school board members and that her job could be in jeopardy. Outwardly, Maheshwari refused to blink: "I simply said that my husband would be glad if I were fired because he believed that I was putting in way too many hours at my work." Shortly afterward, however, she called up other Alliance School principals in other parts of the state for advice. Alejandro Mindiz-Melton of Zavala Elementary School in Austin proved to be especially supportive, and urged her to "trust the organizers." His testimony was important for Maheshwari, for Zavala had improved dramatically after a similar process of community organizing around strongly felt grievances. Maheshwari resolved to keep a steady course, and she also continued to call Mindiz-Melton, who effectively mentored her throughout the organizing process at her school. "I think I talked to him more that year than to many of my colleagues in McAllen," she recalled, "and that's why I always think of the Alliance Schools in the Valley as part of a large, statewide network and not just a local project or program."[10]

Parents, teachers, and Valley Interfaith organizers contacted numerous public officials to come to the assembly—scheduled for February 1995—to commit themselves to improve educational conditions. Public officials such as the chief of police, city council members, the city manager, the superintendent of schools, and school board members were all informed in advance as to the nature of the assembly and the kinds of questions that would be posed to them. When the evening of the Kids' Action Assembly finally arrived, more than three hundred parents from the school attended—a hitherto unprecedented gathering by the community on behalf of its children. Preliminary entertainment was provided by the McAllen High School mariachi band, which helped create an atmosphere of festivity for the people who crowded Sam Houston's cafeteria. The public officials heard parent leaders such as Delia Villarreal, Christina Fuentes, and David Gomez, as well as teachers such as Leticia Casas, Raquel Guzman, and Mary Vela, who described the problems in the neighborhood and asked for their leadership in improving Sam Houston and its community. Speaking in a mixture of Spanish and English, parents and teachers alike committed themselves to working together and to demanding accountability from their civic leaders.

That Kids' Action Assembly played a pivotal role in the history of Sam Houston. For the first time, members of the community saw a host of leaders who were made up of their friends and neighbors seeking a new relationship with public officials and garnering results. As a consequence of the meeting, the city parks and recreation department agreed to fund an after-school program for Sam Houston, which enrolled more than two hundred children in its first year. A police substation was opened closer to the school, and additional officers were assigned to patrol the area. City council members made sure that the trash that filled the alleys near the school was cleaned up and that additional lighting was installed. And to ensure that the community developed its own capacity to improve its children's education, parents at Sam Houston signed a "parent contract" in which parents agreed to ask their children over dinner about their day in school and to insist that homework be done punctually. By May 1995 the school and its community seemed indeed to have turned over a new leaf, and the self-confidence of both the parents and the children seemed to have been enhanced immeasurably. The only issue not substantially addressed concerned the community's hopes for extensive renovations at Sam Houston, if not a brand-new building.

As can so often happen with the uncertain politics of school reform, however, circumstances developed in such a way that a surprise ending awaited those advocating a new building. Just before the Kids' Action Assembly, the McAllen Independent School District hired a new superintendent, Dr. Robert Schumacher. Schumacher inherited a joint plan between the school district, the city of McAllen, and a private corporation called McAllen Affordable Homes to build a new neighborhood that would place home ownership within the grasp of moderate and low-income city residents. Called Los Encinos, the neighborhood was planned several miles south of McAllen proper and would consist of 246 new homes. The school district had committed to construct a brand-new elementary school there, fully equipped with fiber-optic cables to enable students to take full advantage of computer technology.

In January 1996 Schumacher proposed that part of the Sam Houston student body be bused to the new campus and that the remaining children be reassigned to Zavala and Tipton, two elementary schools close to La Paloma. Instantly the community was split about the advantages and disadvantages of the proposal. While many were enthusiastic about the capabilities of the new campus and the prospect that their children would benefit from what appeared to be a state-of-the-art building, others were disappointed at the school's physical distance from its original community and the scattering of the student body to three different campuses. Many parents had enjoyed walking their children to school in the morning and were reluctant to put them on school buses. Some even suggested that the new school was a way to split a community when it had become empowered to advocate successfully for its children. Others, however, pointed out that many other parents in McAllen would be eager to have their children attend the new school and that to squander this opportunity would be a major disservice to the children.

For many months the teachers and parents vacillated about whether to accept or decline Schumacher's proposal. One of the major concerns revolved around what would happen to the old campus if the school was moved, for the campus was situated in the center of La Paloma and played an important role not just as a school but also a place for recreational and leisure activities. One idea that was advanced by Mayor Brand was to tear down the old building and build a new terminal that would receive the major bus lines that run from northern Mexico into the Valley. "All of La Paloma was against that," Estela Sosa-Garza recalled. "They wanted some stability for the community, not a point of transit for hundreds of people moving in and out of the area every day." Yet, what positive use could be made of the old building if La Paloma residents agreed to accept the new campus at Los Encinos?[11]

The next stage of negotiations produced an ingenious solution to the problem of the old campus. For years Valley Interfaith had struggled with the lack of skilled labor in the Valley and watched as professionals such as teachers and nurses were recruited from other parts of the United States while Hidalgo County suffered from unemployment rates sometimes as high as four times the Texas state average. Through conversations with local business leaders and educators at Pan American University, the University of Texas at Brownsville, and Texas State Technical College (in Harlingen), they discovered that the source of the problem was the lack of mediating institutions that could help high school graduates obtain the skills that would lead to specialization and certification in some facet of professional work.

To develop those kinds of institutions, Valley Interfaith launched a program called Project VIDA, which stands for the Valley Initiative for Development and Advancement. Modeled after a similar program called Project QUEST begun by two IAF sister organizations, COPS and the Metro Alliance in San Antonio, Project VIDA targets areas of job growth that provide a living wage (as of this writing, $7.50 an hour, along with health care benefits) and enables individuals to receive the training for those positions. In San Antonio, community colleges exist to provide a broad range of courses for paraprofessionals, but in Hidalgo County, there were no such institutions until Valley Interfaith helped create the South Texas Community College (STCC) in McAllen in 1994.

Valley Interfaith had to fight hard to support the community college initiative in McAllen. When a bond referendum to support the community college was submitted to the public, key community leaders, such as Father Bart of Saint Joseph's and Father Jerry Frank of Holy Spirit Catholic Church, even organized mobile voting units at their churches, so that citizens could take advantage of early voting opportunities and vote on Sunday mornings. "People would proceed directly from Mass into parish halls to vote," Sister Pearl Ceasar recalled, "and that kind of congregationally based organizing was key, because on the actually designated day of the election the bond failed. But because of early voting, we got the community college."[12]

This background information is important to the development of Sam Houston Elementary School because the community college became a key factor in negotiating the transference of the school out of La Paloma to Los Encinos. Valley Interfaith worked successfully with the McAllen superintendent of schools and the president of South Texas Community College to establish a branch campus on the site of the old elementary school. Since enrollment was soaring at STCC—driven by the desire of community residents to acquire the skills that could help them secure better jobs—the community college was desperate for space. Eventually, the school district agreed to lease the campus to the community college for two years, at which point STCC hoped that it would have the funds to begin an extensive program of building renovation.

One last concern that parents had about sending their children to the new campus concerned transportation. Many of the most active parent leaders at the old campus were dependent on public transportation, and there was no way to get from La Paloma to Los Encinos without several transfers on bus lines that ran infrequently. To help them to have a genuine choice to send their children to the new school while maintaining high levels of engagement, parents from the old school received a commitment from the district that it would provide transportation for them to school events. With this condition secured, the parents agreed to accept the move of Sam Houston to the new campus at Los Encinos, which was set to occur during the summer of 1996.

For many educators the most intense phase of struggle at Sam Houston now appeared more or less at an end. La Paloma had garnered a brand-new, wonderfully equipped campus for Sam Houston. Yet the victory was in part Pyrrhic, for only one-fifth of the students on the new campus came from the old Sam Houston; the other students elected to attend neighborhood schools closer to home than to venture six miles south to Los Encinos. Determined to make the most of a difficult situation, Connie Maheshwari struggled to keep up as high a level of parental engagement as possible while ensuring that teachers in the school did all within their power to develop a curriculum that was linked to the community and thus prepare the children to exercise the same kind of civic leadership that had been modeled by their parents. In the two years after Sam Houston's move, Maheshwari and her staff implemented a number of curricular innovations that have sustained an unusually rich relationship between the school and its new, extended community.

One of the intriguing developments that occurred in the school in its new setting was the implementation of a project-based approach to curriculum development. Several teachers at Sam Houston had received training from the McAllen Independent School District on the development of interdisciplinary curricula, and the teachers were eager to use their training to pilot units of study that would be relevant to the children's community. Yet since so many children at the school came from the brand-new neighborhood, it proved somewhat difficult to develop a course of study around a settlement with little of the cultural fabric that develops over time in more established neighborhoods.

The response of the teachers to this curricular dilemma was to engage the students in conversations about their community. Early elementary teachers such as Diana Garza and Raquel Guzman began asking their pupils if they observed anything noteworthy in Los Encinos that they might want to learn more about. The children instantly responded that there was a great deal of housing construction in the community. Observing high levels of student interest in this phenomenon, the teachers asked their pupils if they would like to learn more about how a home is built. When the children responded positively, the teachers began to develop a curriculum that would take the children into the heart of the new neighborhood and would give them a broad range of academic skills that they could apply to a multitude of disciplines.

Diana Garza, a kindergarten teacher, began her project as part of Sam Houston's after-school program. She took the children for walks in the neighborhood and visited some of the homes that were being built directly across the street from the school. Two city housing inspectors, one of whom was the father of a fourth grade pupil at Sam Houston, explained the importance of building well-constructed homes and all of the facets of a home that an inspector must make sure are securely built. Visiting the home repeatedly throughout the fall of 1996, the children observed the workers pouring concrete, framing and roofing the house, and installing plumbing and electricity. In the classroom, Garza had the students mix water with clay to replicate the process that a mason uses mixing water with sand to make mortar or concrete, and they developed their artistic skills drawing homes in different stages of development. Students then used a variety of materials to make their own small-scale homes. "It was a good way to tie the community with the school," Garza recalled. "There's nothing like firsthand experience. But the best thing was that the kids learned a lot."[13]

First grade teacher Raquel Guzman decided to explore a project on construction as part of her regular classroom instruction. Once she had inquired whether the children would like to learn more about building homes, she worked with the school librarian to acquire books on construction, plumbing, and electricity, and she asked the foreman of construction across the street from the school if he would be willing to talk with the children about his work. When the foreman obliged, he discovered that the children had many questions that he could only explain with difficulty without visual reference to a new home. He then invited the class to go with him to the construction site, where he explained all of the planning and skill that must go into building a house.

"These children had question after question," Guzman commented, and she used the children's motivation to develop a rich interdisciplinary curriculum that wove together reading, writing, and mathematics. Teams of students began keeping logs about the different stages of home construction, and they learned to spell vocabulary words such as "cement," "shingle," "insulation," and "power gun." The workers on the construction site enjoyed showing the children the work they were doing, and Guzman believes they took special pride in having the opportunity to showcase their skills to the students.[14]

Raquel Guzman was particularly intrigued to observe the way that the project on construction catalyzed the learning of children who previously were marginal in their academic achievement. She noted that one particular student usually needed extra attention when it came to reading, writing, or mathematics. Guzman admired his tenacious efforts to succeed academically, but she also observed that his struggles to master the regular curriculum were damaging his confidence. Once the project on home construction began, however, "He lit up. He was always the first one who knew all of the new vocabulary, while he usually wasn't so confident because he hadn't been a strong reader and always needed extra help. I was so surprised with him, and he's made much more of a connection to me. Best of all, the new skills he has learned have spread to the other academic areas and the other kids now see him as a real class leader."[15]

Guzman observed that the construction project has also helped the children to make stronger connections to their own community, even if they are bused to the new campus from the old Sam Houston neighborhood. "A lot of these kids have parents who work in construction or other blue-collar jobs," Guzman noted, "and the parents have brought it up in parent-teacher meetings that the construction unit has been a real hit with the kids." Traveling to a museum in McAllen for a field trip, Guzman noticed the children shouting with delight as they passed by new-home construction and identified all of the different tasks that were being accomplished. She has used the children's interests to open up the professional world to them. "I've told them about architects, and how architects use reading, writing, and math to design their new houses, and that seemed to give them some extra connection and motivation to achieve with their schoolwork," she commented.[16]

A second area in which Sam Houston has developed innovative approaches to education is in the area of civics. Shortly after moving to the new campus, Connie Maheshwari learned about a "microsociety" project developed at Jacobson Elementary School in Las Vegas, Nevada. She took a group of teachers and parents to visit Jacobson in the summer of 1997 and was impressed by a school which enabled students to try out a number of civic roles in an extended, schoolwide simulation. In a nutshell, the project enables students to be elected to serve as the mayor, treasurer, planner, parliamentarian, or recorder of their campus, and provides for the establishment of a bank and a mock "Target" store run by students and monitored by teachers. The project not only creates these new social roles for students but also gives guidelines for the very real altercations that arise when individuals enter an explicitly political arena. "I was so amazed at Jacobson," teacher Raquel Guzman said, "because I saw kids that had real social roles in the school and they were so confident about what they were doing. I thought that it would be so great if we could give those same life skills to our kids, and I know we can do it." The new mayor of McAllen, Leo Montalvo, visited the new campus in the fall of 1997 and spoke at length with the campus mayor, a confident fifth grader named Robert Garza.[17]

As one should anticipate with any venture as bold as the microsociety undertaking, numerous problems occurred with implementation in the first two years. Some students took the "Cougar Cash" money that was used in the microsociety and made photocopies of it to acquire copies of the toys sold in the campus Target store; store managers embezzled the cash; the bank tellers had problems with recordkeeping and one student claimed that she needed a lawyer because the bank claimed that she had less money than she was sure that she had deposited. In each of these instances, Sam Houston teachers worked with students to point out that these problems reflect problems that happen in real life and to come up with solutions to keep the microsociety afloat. Some of the incidents did create tensions between teachers and students; thus, Mary Vela, one of the chief architects of the microsociety, not only discovered the embezzling of "Cougar cash" in her fourth grade classroom, but she had to initiate the follow-through so that the managers were dismissed from their positions.

In addition, the problems with breaking rules created an awareness among students and faculty that they needed to devise a judicial system. By the fall of 1999 Sam Houston began creating a court system for the microsociety. As part of that venture, teachers not only taught students vocabulary about bailiffs, prosecutors, and defense attorneys, but they also invited in a judge, a lawyer, and a police officer to talk about the nature of their work so that students could understand what kind of work they would be accepting if they chose to play these roles in the microsociety. Students prepared questions for the professionals—which included everything from how much money they made to why they chose their profession—and engaged Ed Aparisio (a judge), Eddie Anaya (a lawyer), and Lucas Torres (a police officer and the father of a Sam Houston student) in animated discussion about their work and its positive and negative features.

Third, the civic engagement of Sam Houston teachers and parents has been transmitted to the students through curriculum development in social studies classes. In the fall of 1997 teachers Leticia Casas, Mary

Vela, Susanna Sarmiento, and Mary Ann Rosales taught fourth and fifth graders about an upcoming school bond election, scheduled for 4 October. The students were taught about the issues at stake in the election in order to prepare them to venture forth into the community to inform neighborhood residents about the referendum. As part of the preparation, students met in small groups and wrote out exactly what they would say to community members in both Spanish and English. Following role-play procedures that teachers had learned from Valley Interfaith organizer Estela Sosa-Garza in preparation for the Kids' Action Assembly, students read from their scripts and entertained possible responses from the community so that they would be ready to answer questions in an informed and accurate way.

The fourth grade classes did their community excursion on the Friday before the referendum, going door-to-door with parents and teachers to inform residents about the upcoming election; the fifth grade students went with their teachers on the Saturday of the referendum. Speaking in both Spanish and English, the students informed the community that even though they would not be direct beneficiaries at Sam Houston, the bond election would benefit students at other schools in McAllen. "It was our school picture day, so we were all dressed up when we went out," said Sarai Oviedo, a fifth grader, "and it was a lot more fun than just sitting at our desks doing our usual school stuff." Fifth grade teacher Mary Ann Rosales said, "I was very proud of my students, because when people asked them why they cared about taxes for improving schools when they already had the newest school in the district, the students were ready to say that they wanted all of the children in McAllen to have a school as good as theirs." Voter turnout went up dramatically in Los Encinos on 4 October, with 188 votes cast in the 234-home neighborhood, and the bond issue passed. "We never had these kinds of learning opportunities when I was growing up," teacher Leticia Casas commented. "These kids are getting a chance to see themselves as a real part of this community."[18]

A fourth manner in which Sam Houston has changed its culture concerns its resourcefulness in regard to utilizing the talents of parents as curriculum developers. Continuing the tradition of house meetings begun at the time of the Kids' Action Assembly, teachers have met with parents on a regular basis in their homes to discuss innovative course materials that they could design together for the students. One immigrant mother, Eusebia Hinojosa, expended tremendous energy to prepare Sam Houston for a celebration of Mexican independence day—el 16 de septiembre—in the late summer of 1997. Hinojosa rallied a group of other parents around her, sought out curriculum materials on the Mexican side of the border, and taught classes that demonstrated folk art and indigenous dance traditions to the children.

Excited by the growing relationship with parents as curriculum developers, teachers continued to meet with parents in their homes in the ensuing months to discuss additional opportunities for pedagogical collaborations. Working together, the parents and teachers decided to develop a curriculum unit on the posada, a traditional Mexican ceremony in which community members dress up as Joseph and Mary (José and Maria) and wander from one home to another, gathering followers and singing Christmas carols. The posada allows individuals to identify with the quest of Joseph and Mary and provides an important form of social cohesion to a community. As part of the preparation for the posada, Eusebia Hinojosa took the teachers to the public library in Reynosa, Mexico, and acted as a de facto tour guide and cultural interlocutor for the teachers. When the teachers returned they worked with a larger group of parents who offered the children a wonderful neighborhood excursion in which children sang the songs of the posada and visited mothers in their kitchens in their homes. Mothers not only served the children homemade *ponche caliente, posole, buñuelos, champurrados,* and tamales, but also taught the children about the recipes that they used and the significance of particular foods and drinks in their culture. At the end of the outing children returned not only to demolish a piñata and to relish the candies packed therein, but also to learn about the significance of the piñata's five points, which refer to five different sins that the children attack when they hit the piñata. "What was so neat was that the instruction really happened out in the community," Mary Vela enthused. Through these kinds of activities the mothers expanded the horizons of the teachers, provided the children with information about Mexican culture and their folk heritage, and modeled a rich collaborative relationship between home, school, and community.[19]

Ostensibly, one might anticipate that the work entailed in creating joint curricular units between teachers and parents could be construed as an additional (and unwanted) burden by teachers. Yet the teachers themselves deny that this is the case. "When I myself first started teaching eleven years ago, I did the curriculum that was set out for me, even though it wasn't really what I wanted to do," fifth grade teacher Mary Ann Rosales said. "It wasn't until six years ago, when I first came to Sam Houston, that I saw that I really could do so much more, and that it could be so much more powerful. I always wanted to find ways to involve parents and the community, but nobody taught me that at the university. But now, through the Alliance Schools, and because Connie [Maheshwari] gives us so much leeway to do what we want, I see that we can give the children so much more, and that it changes a school into a place where the children really want to go. And because I have two children in Sam Houston myself, I know that it makes all of the difference in the world."[20]

As a result of these developments, Sam Houston Elementary has developed a self-sustaining momentum in regard to school-community collaboration in which parents and teachers meet on a regular basis to develop culturally responsive pedagogies that will enable the children to hold on to key facets of traditional Mexican culture at the same time that they acquire the civic skills that will allow them to participate in the political arena in the United States. Mothers such as Eusebia Hinojosa, Irma Hernandez, Monserrat Herrera, Maria Hernandez, Diana Salinas, and Lucia Gonzalez have worked with teachers to develop curricular units celebrating el Día de los Muertos, el Día de los Reyes, and el Día de la Candelaria, all of which are Mexican cultural holidays that fuse indigenous and Christian religious practices.

Through all of these different efforts, Sam Houston is finding myriad pedagogical channels to sustain and enliven the organizing efforts that began in 1994 and that reconstituted the school as a civic center for its community. Although the process of relocating the campus on the far southern edge of McAllen was contested, teachers, students, and parents have found ways to work together that have engendered new curricular units, developed the role of parents as pedagogical innovators, and taught students the fundamentals of civic engagement. In addition to all of this educational ferment, the teachers have also sought to be realistic and to link students' learning, whenever possible, to the skills that are measured on the TAAS. Thus, teachers helped them summarize newspaper articles on the bond referendum in a manner similar to that which appears on the TAAS; students wrote about the posada in a fashion that helped them monitor and reflect critically on their own learning; and fourth grade teachers Leticia Casas and Mary Vela gave math exercises based on transportation to Valley Interfaith's fifteenth anniversary convention. "We don't completely detach ourselves from TAAS objectives," Connie Maheshwari said. "In fact, we work very hard on the problem-solving skills that are needed for the test. We just do it differently."[21]

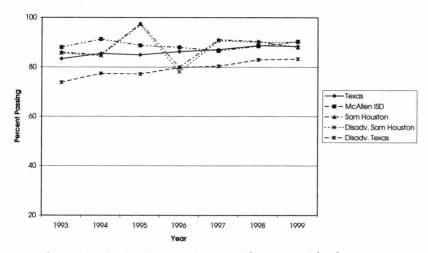

Grade 4 TAAS Writing Test, Sam Houston Elementary School, 1994–1999.

That gamble—the wager that one could both develop a full range of pedagogical and curricular innovations and prepare students to do well on the TAAS—is one that few educators in Texas have been willing to take in recent years. The costs of doing poorly on the TAAS have simply been too high to allow educators much margin for error while exploring new approaches to teaching and learning. Yet Sam Houston was to experience a different and more felicitous outcome when it received its TAAS scores in the spring of 1998, and the faculty learned that the school achieved exemplary test scores on the TAAS from the Texas Education Agency. The school outperformed not only the district averages at each grade level but also Texas state averages for all assessments of reading and mathematics except for those of fourth grade math. In addition, economically disadvantaged students at Sam Houston dramatically outperformed the comparison group of economically disadvantaged students across Texas at each grade level. While all of the educational ferment on the campus, in the community, and in the relationship with Saint Joseph's the Worker was intrinsically important, it was an additional source of satisfaction to know that the work had also paid off in terms of standardized test results.

The appendix provides an overview of Sam Houston's progress on the TAAS from 1993 to 1999. Sam Houston's scores show an upward trajectory in achievement on the reading and mathematics sections of the TAAS from 1993 to 1998. Even when Sam Houston students' scores began at a level that exceeded both district and state scores—as was the case for third graders in both reading and mathematics—they generally continued their strong performances across those years.

This same high level of achievement also held for the fourth grade students on the writing section of the TAAS. With the single exception of 1996, disadvantaged Sam Houston fourth graders outperformed the aggregate of disadvantaged Texas fourth graders by a wide margin. Given the concentrated nature of poverty in the South McAllen barrios that Sam Houston serves, this achievement seems particularly noteworthy.

Aside from these positive findings, however, the data also reveal two areas of concern. In spite of Sam Houston's emphasis on cultural responsiveness, its students had more trouble on the Spanish-language TAAS than other students in the same cohort at the district and the state level. If Sam Houston's teachers want to raise those scores, they may need to pay less attention to cultural influences and instead focus more specifically on linguistic capabilities or test-taking skills. The challenge in this case would be to find a way to conserve the sense of excitement about learning that culturally congruent pedagogy and curricula enable while at the same time ensuring that the students have the skills that will promote their achievement on standardized tests.

The second major area of concern relates to the slump in scores at the third and fifth grade levels from 1998 to 1999 in both reading and mathematics, but especially in reading. Only the fourth grade students outperformed their peers in reading and mathematics at the state and district level in 1999. As a consequence of these results, Sam Houston's rating by the Texas Education Agency fell from exemplary to recognized in 1999.

As was the case with our test score analyses from Palmer and Alamo, it is difficult to know why the scores developed as they have at Sam Houston. At least part of the outcome may be related to changes in student population, such as the increase of third graders in Sam Houston in 1999, when enrollment moved from 42 to 67 students in a single year. When queried, Connie Maheshwari was upbeat. "It means we have to work harder," she said. "It doesn't mean that our kids don't know the answers to the questions on the test. I think it's more likely that they might have been unfamiliar with the format. Sometimes slight differences in wording or presentation can make a big difference for a child."[22]

CHAPTER FIVE

THE CHALLENGES OF COMMUNITY ORGANIZING AND SCHOOL REFORM

In the last fifteen years Valley Interfaith helped effect a number of changes in the Lower Rio Grande Valley that have had a significant impact on community leadership, conditions in the colonias, and school reform. The Lower Valley remains a region of disproportionately high poverty, however, and even though improvements have been made in the colonias and in the schools that serve them, many challenges remain. While gangs might play a minimal role in the school cultures at Palmer, Alamo, and Sam Houston, they are still strong in the surrounding communities. Even when teachers pay home visits, their contacts are usually too fleeting to transform situations in which wives are abused by husbands or families are evicted due to their inability to pay the rent. School personnel—whether teachers, counselors, or principals —face a daunting uphill struggle when they endeavor to improve community conditions in addition to their regular instructional load so that children have a better chance of mastering their school's curriculum.

In spite of the challenges, however, it appears clear that the Alliance School initiative is slowly changing the culture of schooling in the Valley. In addition to the three schools described above, all of which helped initiate the Alliance School effort in the Lower Border, twenty other schools have joined to create new kinds of horizontal ties between schools and churches in the region. The complex ensemble of community organizing strategies taught by Valley Interfaith—from individual conversations to house meetings to neighborhood walks to accountability sessions—add an intriguing new piece to the mosaic of contemporary school reform and community development.

By reconceptualizing the process of schooling and actualizing a specific model of civic engagement, the Alliance School network emphasizes joint strategies of school reform and community improvement. Yet the contribution of the Alliance Schools is not merely conceptual. From 1995 to 1999 the schools that were Alliance Schools in the Valley at that time acquired more than $500,000 from funds allocated by the Texas Legislature to the broader network—and those funds were badly needed. At Palmer, Alamo, and Sam Houston, they were allocated for staff development, after-school programs, peer mediation, and parent education programs. The increasing allocation of funds from the legislature to Alliance Schools in the Valley would appear to make their work easier. At the same time, the new schools will also have to make sure that they do not allow the lure of money to detract from the labor entailed in home visits, house meetings, and other forms of community engagement.[1]

How successful can we really say the three schools that we have studied above have been? The answer is not at all straightforward. As measured by TAAS data, the portrait is an uneven one. Palmer began with high levels of achievement and has generally struggled to maintain those, while the rates of progress in the district, in the state, and among disadvantaged students at the state level have been higher. Alamo began with low scores and has made steady progress over the six years measured in this account. Sam Houston is the only one of the schools to have reached the highest levels of achievement and to warrant an exemplary rating by the Texas Education Agency in 1998, but that accomplishment was short lived, as scores fell in the subsequent year.

How much weight should be placed on these scores? Psychometricians are divided about the validity and reliability of high-stakes tests like the TAAS. On the one hand, numerous critics have pointed out what appear to be serious flaws in the TAAS. One analysis of the TAAS by mathematicians Paul Clopton, Wayne Bishop, and David Klein argued that Texas students could pass the TAAS math exit exam for high school graduation and still have difficulty with a test widely administered to twelve-year-olds in Japan. Another study by reading specialist Sandra Stotsky argued that in recent years the TAAS test designers have created easier questions for students. The results of three surveys that have been administered to teachers in Texas reveal that teachers consider the TAAS to be inimical in many ways to sound educational practices. Finally, Walter Haney, in a deposition for the Mexican American Legal Defense and Education Fund against the Texas Education Agency, noted that although the state of Texas holds all students to the same standards for high school graduation on the TAAS exit test, it has not presented evidence that it has provided students (and particularly minorities) with an equal education as part of the preparation for that test.[2]

On the other hand, defenders of the TAAS contend that whatever its problems and unintended social consequences, the test has played a major role in improving the academic achievement of Texas youngsters. Supporters of the TAAS point to the high gains of Texas students on the National Assessment of Educational Progress (NAEP), generally recognized as the instrument with the best reliability and validity for measuring student achievement across the fifty states. Researchers at the Charles A. Dana Center at the University of Texas at Austin have compiled NAEP data pertaining to Texas students on their website, and on the whole the data are impressive. It is difficult to observe that African American fourth graders are first in the nation in mathematics on the NAEP among their cohort, and Title I participants are first among theirs, without conceding that something positive must be occurring in the Lone Star State to generate those results. The Dana Center has been particularly effective at documenting the manner in which Texas children participating in free- or reduced-lunch programs, or coming from households in which parents are not high school graduates, have exceeded expectations in terms of their academic achievement on the NAEP. Other researchers, from groups as diverse as the Education Trust, the National Education Goals Panel, and the Heritage Foundation have endorsed the testing strategies that have evolved in Texas as worthy of national emulation.[3]

Given the intensity of debate among assessment experts and policy analysts about the benefits and problems of high-stakes tests such as the TAAS, it seems prudent to view the TAAS as one resource that can provide educators with information about student achievement, and to augment that information with ethnographic data. This is particularly critical in an account such as this one, where the field of study is not student achievement per se but the nexus between community organizing and school reform. In addition, the Rio Grande Valley is a distinctive cultural area, characterized by high rates of migration from Mexico and a significant minority of migrant workers who leave the Valley with their families in the spring and return in the autumn after the crops have been harvested each year. Once we widen the lens to accommodate this context and to formulate a larger inquiry that addresses the mutual development of schools and communities, how might we evaluate the trajectories of the three schools studied above?

In reviewing the schools, it might appear that Sam Houston has risked the most and had the most success in engaging the community on a *pedagogical* level. At Sam Houston, civic engagement has fused with student learning in a number of ways. The school has conducted research into housing construction in Los Encinos, created a microsociety with a mayor and town commissioners, and sponsored field trips informing adults about the issues that would be addressed in an upcoming school bond referendum. Sam Houston reveals in a most salient fashion how schools can create a curriculum of civic education that dissolves the boundaries between the school and the community and educates both students and adults about issues that are at stake in their immediate future. When seen against the larger backdrop of the crime and neighborhood deterioration that occurred in La Paloma, the transformation of Sam Houston Elementary School is a provocative demonstration of how dramatic the changes can be when parents are fully engaged in actualizing the potential embedded in their children's schools and communities.

This favorable interpretation must be advanced in light of the very different community context of Sam Houston vis-à-vis Palmer and Alamo. Recall that Sam Houston is now in a new school building which is located in a new housing development (Los Encinos), and that only one-fifth of the students from the original neighborhood (La Paloma) followed the teachers to the new building. Although one cannot know for sure, one can speculate that the parents who moved into the new housing development might be better connected socially and demonstrate higher levels of household organization than the parents in Las Milpas in Pharr, which served Palmer, or the colonias serving Alamo. Connie Maheshwari herself recognized this when she said shortly after the school's opening, "We'd better get an exemplary rating on the TAAS, with this perfect new building completely wired with fiber-optic cables." Thus, housing capital and technology capital—as well as the marketplace factors entailed in parents' decision to move out of older barrios to Los Encinos—all could play powerful roles in assisting Sam Houston's trajectory.[4]

Yet even given those two important caveats—pertaining to the reliability of the TAAS and the different community context in Los Encinos—Sam Houston's achievement still appears striking and not at all self-evident. What explains the level of civic engagement and pedagogical creativity at Sam Houston when compared to the developments at Palmer or Alamo? Palmer, after all, enjoys the leadership of a talented and deeply committed principal, and Alamo has undergone a number of transformations that have propelled it out of complete chaos into being a school that, while still struggling, has improved test scores and achieved an overall atmosphere of purposeful learning.

Any number of factors can be seen as important here; key considerations include the more dispersed populations in the colonias of Pharr and Alamo, the varying talent of teachers, the quality of district leadership, and last but not least, differences in the students themselves. Working with Valley Interfaith, the colonias in Pharr and Alamo have developed considerable civic leadership, and the teachers at Palmer and Alamo appear to be just as hardworking and talented as the teachers at Sam Houston. Bill Morgan, the superintendent of schools in Pharr–San Juan–Alamo, is an outspoken champion of the Alliance Schools, while Robert Schumacher, the McAllen superintendent who oversees Sam Houston, appears to be more reserved; certainly the Alliance Schools in McAllen have not enjoyed the explicit recruitment, transportation, and funding support afforded the Alliance Schools in Pharr–San Juan–Alamo. All of the schools serve populations made up almost exclusively of Mexican American children of low and moderate income. What might explain the differences?

Reviewing the three case studies presented above, one of the most striking contrasts between the developments at Palmer and Alamo compared to Sam Houston concerns the powerful accumulation of *social capital* that Sam Houston has evidenced. Recall that Sam Houston has enjoyed unusually strong civic leadership from Saint Joseph's the Worker Catholic Church, while the involvement of the churches in Pharr and Alamo has been relatively peripheral to the Alliance School effort. Salvador Flores first heard of Valley Interfaith through a fellow parishioner at Saint Margaret's in Pharr, and parents at Alamo held meetings at Resurrection Catholic Church when the school was in danger of losing its sixth grade pupils and teachers, but otherwise the churches have refrained from civic leadership around issues of school reform and community development.

This situation could hardly be more apposite for Sam Houston Elementary School. Even before Sam Houston became an Alliance School, Father Bart Flaat and Sister Maria Sánchez had established *comunidades de base,* conducted house meetings, and taught the citizens and immigrants in La Paloma a wide range of strategies to help them improve neighborhood security, agitate for health care and job training, and register to vote. Father Bart announced Valley Interfaith events during Mass on Sundays, and the church provided transportation for its members when they needed to come to meetings in other parts of McAllen or the Valley. Likewise, Father Bart and Sister Maria had already set up and attended numerous meetings with public officials and with their parishioners and had established an identity as the flagship institution in McAllen that supported Valley Interfaith's approach to civic engagement. When Connie Maheshwari then began the process of community organizing for school reform, she was *extending* a process that had strong institutional support from Saint Joseph's into the culture of her school rather than *introducing* it.

In this context it is particularly important to understand the role of the Catholic Church in the immigrant and Mexican American communities in the Valley. "Here the church is the center of their lives," Sister Pearl Ceasar observed. "That's different here than in more urban areas." Jim Drake, the first lead organizer for Valley Interfaith who had spent seventeen years working with the United Farm Workers, was astonished at the depth of religious conviction in the Valley. "Religious *belief* shapes everything in the Valley, in a way that I have not experienced before except for the brief time I was in India," he wrote in 1986. "Belief in the Virgin and in Jesus, in that order, runs this place." Immigrants might be intimidated by schools, and they might be terrified of the police and immigration officials, but they find a source of continuity and identity in the church, its liturgy, and its congregation. In addition, Father Bart noted that "in Mexico, it is common for there to be a close relationship between the Catholic Church and the schools in the community. This means that if immigrants see us [at Saint Joseph's] working together with the schools, they don't think of it as anything unusual." In other words, Saint Joseph's and Sam Houston, through their collaboration, exhibit a powerful kind of *cultural congruence* between key community institutions for the families they serve.[5]

We now can specify one reason for the unusually high level of civic engagement that has developed at Sam Houston. In a nutshell, Saint Joseph's the Worker provided a specific kind of social capital to Sam Houston that neither Palmer nor Alamo enjoyed, at least to the same degree. In this instance, that social capital entailed the textured relationships and access to political and economic power that a religious institution can bring to a population of low-income, Spanish-monolingual immigrants and citizens who need mentoring and training to develop their civic capacities. Whether through *comunidades de base*, house meetings, its parish convention, or its involvement in Sam Houston's transformation, Saint Joseph's has energetically pursued social capitalization in its efforts to improve health, safety, and job training in South McAllen. And the linkages between Saint Joseph's and Sam Houston are not restricted to isolated programs; they are actualizations of long-term relationships that have accrued over time to become part of the texture of everyday life for community leaders. As she has for many years, Connie Maheshwari continues to teach classes leading toward confirmation at an auxiliary of Saint Joseph's, La Capilla, and Sister Maria Sánchez is on Sam Houston's shared-decision-making team; both women are strong leaders with Valley Interfaith. They exemplify *bridging* social capital—those relationships between individuals that establish strong horizontal ties across institutional lines.

Of noteworthy importance in these bridging relationships is the civic power of women, whether they be Mexican immigrants or Mexican American citizens. This observation is worth underlining because of a widespread stereotype about the persistence of a particularly predatory kind of patriarchy in Mexican-immigrant and Mexican American households. Scholars such as Maxine Baca Zinn, Alfredo Mirandé, Evangelina Enríquez, and Carlos Vélez-Ibáñez have all demonstrated that while patriarchy certainly plays a powerful role in Mexican-descent households, women enjoy dense and reciprocal social relationships with one another that consolidate family ties, allow them important influence over domestic financial decisions, and sacralize everyday life through ritual cycles of exchange. In addition, an important recent contribution by Pierette Hondagenu-Sotelo has demonstrated that the process of immigration into the United States plays a much more influential role in empowering Mexican-descent women than has hitherto been recognized. At issue is neither the adaptation of Mexican-descent women to Anglo society nor contact with feminist theory, both of which are considerably removed from the relatively segregated jobs and well-defined immigrant and Mexican American communities in which the women work and live. Rather, the processes of immigration and settlement appear to erode subtly traditional Mexican patterns of patriarchy by expanding women's economic contributions to the family and increasing their decision-making capacities in relationship to school, church, and other social institutions.[6]

In addition to illuminating the potential of Mexican-descent women to develop their civic capacity around matters of educational reform and community improvement, the case of Sam Houston and Saint Joseph's indicates something of the paradoxical role of the Catholic Church in each of these domains as well. Although Church doctrine is in many ways repressive of women's leadership development—particularly in terms of prohibitions on liturgical participation and the holding of church offices—it nonetheless remains true that both the social networks that the Church sustains and the theological and moral dimension of Catholicism provide powerful frameworks for the development of women's civic capacity. This paradoxical facet of the Church—which can easily be overlooked but has long been noted by Latina feminist theologians—can become remarkably generative in both theory and practice in the work of community organizing for school reform. For if one combines recognition of women's leadership development in the Church with the predominance of women in schools as teachers and parent activists—and if one understands that these relationships are in many ways overlapping and mutually sustaining—then a theoretical groundwork is laid in which Mexican-descent women can use these networks to develop advocacy on behalf of their children and families through a broad-based organization such as Valley Interfaith.[7]

Thus, one major difference between Sam Houston and Alamo and Palmer resides in the unusually strong *bridging* social capital that has been forged between women at Saint Joseph's the Worker and the elementary school. Yet it would be a mistake to see that social network dimension of Sam Houston's identity as the sole cause of the school's achievements. An equally important contribution may be assigned to the transformation of teachers' culture at Sam Houston. For while teachers at Palmer and Alamo have been involved in a host of pedagogical reforms—such as the introduction of two-way bilingual education, the development of a culture of home visits that focus on children's social and cognitive development, and the formation of teacher teams—none of these innovations seem to have reached the depth of the place-based curriculum achieved by the teachers at Sam Houston.

Recall that teachers at Sam Houston have recognized the spiritual dimension of education through activities related to Mexican religious and cultural holidays, the community-building aspect of education through the construction project and the 16 de septiembre celebration; and the civic facet of education through the school board referendum and the microsociety. Yet more important than any of these particular initiatives is the fact that the teachers have developed a self-sustaining culture of critical inquiry that continually manifests the latent ties existing between a school and its community. The teachers have deliberately sought to develop the pedagogical talents of parents, even when their immigrant and Spanish-monolingual status might easily relegate them to the periphery of many school communities.

Through these multiple kinds of audacious pedagogical ventures, the teachers at Sam Houston have transformed their work from that of passive transmitters of state curricular frameworks or coaches for the TAAS into genuine intellectual activists. They have actualized their capacities in ways that bear affinities to both Henry Giroux's scholarship on "teachers as intellectuals" and Marilyn Cochran-Smith and Susan Lytle's articulation of "teachers as researchers." In both conceptualizations, teachers develop a heightened sense of agency and efficacy, reconstruct the knowledge in their field in ways that deepen their ties to students and their communities, and nourish horizontal ties with other teachers within their institution that promote continued inquiry into and renewal of their work. By doing so, the teachers have moved beyond the kind of "defensive teaching" that Linda McNeil has documented in which teachers feel compelled to defend the culture of school bureaucracies even while recognizing that they are shortchanging the authentic growth and development of their students. Instead they have properly insisted on developing the academic capacities of students in a manner that cultivates respect for students' home cultures, uses those cultures as a basis for curriculum development and intellectual inquiry, and promotes students' overall psychological and social development.[8]

These reflections are salient to our line of study at this point because it seems clear that one particular ramification of Alliance School culture—in the Rio Grande Valley and elsewhere in Texas—is to call into question the framing of teachers as "professionals" apart from the communities they serve. Rather, the complex matrix of Alliance School "actions"—from "one-on-one's" to neighborhood walks to accountability sessions—aims to develop new forms of horizontal ties that link teachers with parents, religious institutions, and community-based organizations in a rich web of relationships. The teachers themselves are aware of their transformation and growth through their new ties to parents and their communities. In a letter written in response to a question about their role at Sam Houston Elementary, teachers Leticia Cases, Mary Vela, and Susanna Sarmiento wrote:

> No, we have not always taught this way. First, we had many conversations with Valley Interfaith organizers such as Estela, Sister Pearl, Father Bart, Ernie Cortés, Connie, and each other. In those conversations we were agitated. In fact quite a bit. These

conversations got us to think about relationships and power. We recognized that we did not have relationships to the parents that were meaningful for the overall achievement of the students. The more we thought about it, the more we realized that we needed to change. The first step in this change happened at the old Sam Houston through the first house meetings. We started to deal with issues that were important to our parents. The issues were serious ones—safety and others. Working with the parents on these issues made us see the parents as allies.

Today, we find that working in isolation like so many teachers is not for us. We find that collaborating with each other is more effective for student learning. We now believe that education is the responsibility of not only the teacher but also administrators, parents, and community members. This belief has encouraged us to involve the parents as well as the community in the education of their children. We discovered that parents have so much to contribute. We have learned so much from each other.

In these remarks, Casas, Vela, and Sarmiento describe the link between the school and the community and strengthened ties between teachers within the school as part of a unified pattern of educational growth and development. For these teachers it has become an unspoken assumption of their daily instruction and curriculum development that parents are powerful resources who can help to leverage their children's education in a close network of horizontal ties between the school and the home.[9]

Understanding the achievement of Casas, Vela, and Sarmiento, and the differences between the development of teachers as researchers and more orthodox professional roles is a matter of no small import in the politics and sociology of education in the current historical moment. To appreciate the difference, it is helpful to refer to an article by Julie White and Gary Wehlage entitled "Community Collaboration: If It Is Such a Good Idea, Why Is It So Hard to Do?" White and Wehlage refer to an ambitious effort launched by the Annie E. Casey Foundation called the New Futures Initiative, which aimed to increase high school graduation rates, reduce teenage pregnancies, and increase youth employment after high school in six cities. In brief, New Futures failed. In considering the many reasons why, White and Wehlage made a key finding: New Futures essentially failed to consider the social nature of the clients that it sought to serve. "Institutionally delivered social services are designed around assumptions about the need to develop autonomous individuals, who with help are expected to become more independent, self-reliant, and responsible," they wrote. "Largely ignored is the need to build strong connections among people to enhance their capacity as social individuals to engage in collective, interdependent action." White and Wehlage proceeded to suggest that social capital theory, with its emphasis on common norms and social networks, provides an alternative strategy for conceptualizing and promoting the interests of at-risk youth. The implication is that educators must first recognize that their students are embedded in social networks—particularly their families, but also religious institutions, sports clubs, and other secondary associations—and then use those networks as fulcrums for enhancing their educational opportunities.[10]

A host of consequences ensue from these reflections. At the very least, educators may use this analysis as a point of departure for exploring anew and building upon latent relationships among themselves, their students, and their communities. A bolder stance would be to take seriously the conjoint strategy of school and community renewal and develop schools as centers of civic engagement. In the latter case, educators must be forewarned that some discomfort is likely to be an inevitable concomitant of this variant of school reform. In the case of the Alliance Schools in the Rio Grande Valley, neighborhood walks and home visits subvert the dominant culture of schools as exclusive sites for the inculcation of knowledge by placing teachers in immediate relationship to students' lives outside of school. A teacher at Alamo Middle School who visited the homes of pupils commented on this tension: "You're sitting at school worried about the TAAS and then you get out into the community, visit a student that you've been pounding on in class, and see that he doesn't even have a bed to sleep on—and all the while in class you've been after him to buy books. Or you visit a student who lives in a school bus and whose mother runs an extension cord over to a neighbor's house to get electricity. Then you wonder what we're really doing here."

It is important to note that teachers' experiences of this kind could be barren of results without a larger community of inquiry and practice to promote reflection *and* to link that reflection with forms of social action similar to those developed by Valley Interfaith. The interpretation of experience—in this context—is more important than the experience itself. After all, teachers could visit students' homes, discover the material poverty of the conditions, and decide to lower academic

standards out of a misplaced sense of sympathy; it is an entirely different response to identify a problem and then to work with the community to improve living conditions in a manner exemplified by Salvador
Flores, Carmen Anaya, and the teachers and parents at Palmer Elementary School. Similarly, work with a parish such as Saint Joseph's on
issues of school reform and community development falls outside the
boundaries of most of the dominant rhetoric of "professional development" and indicates just how removed our concepts of professionalism
have become from the emphasis on active citizenry that has been the
foundation of American concepts of liberty, however much they have
fluctuated over time.[11]

In the interests of clarity, it is worth underlining that most American teachers are working very hard, and it is also important to note that
many have extended themselves to forge ties with parents. Yet it also
must be recognized that most of those ties with the community generally have not resulted in curricular units, developed by teachers and
parents together, that instantiate the fusion of school and community
on a *pedagogical* level that is immediately salient to children. The teachers at Sam Houston Elementary School who developed a curriculum
unit on the posada were tapping into the (generally neglected) resource
that anthropologists Luis Moll and James Greenberg have described as
"household funds of knowledge," which can facilitate cultural congruence between the home and the school. In this instance, parents developed an educational identity that was based physically in the home
and in which mothers' kitchens became transformed into innovative
pedagogical laboratories in a manner that was directly accessible for the
children.[12]

The contrast between this kind of parental engagement that builds
social capital and other more traditional models is significant. As scholars as diverse as Joyce Epstein, Concha Delgado-Gaitan, James Comer,
Sarah Lawrence Lightfoot, Lawrence Steinberg, and Seymour Sarason
have noted, there are many different kinds of parental involvement, and
their payoff in terms of children's learning varies widely. Some forms—
such as support for sports activities, field trips to amusement parks,
or governance issues far removed from instruction—may even distract
from and unintentionally undermine the teaching and learning mission
of schools. Other forms of parental involvement help develop children's
learning, but do not recognize the particular needs for cultural congruence between school and the home that are important for poor and minority children. It appears to be Sam Houston's fortune to have devel-

oped a combination of strengths—from the bridging social capital ties to Saint Joseph's, to the continual development of innovative curricular units in collaboration with parents—that result in inventive and compelling curricula for children.[13]

The role that is played by Valley Interfaith in this context is both subtle and powerful. The organization is not omnipresent on campuses and its role is contested, particularly at Alamo. Oppositional teachers at Alamo resented Valley Interfaith for agitating the teachers to engage the community when teachers felt that their efforts were better spent on specifically instructional matters. For the teachers, social capitalization between the school and the community represented a distraction from their specifically academic mission and represented what might be termed a "hidden cost" of social capital. In addition, the teachers questioned the role of the school administration in promoting the collaboration with Valley Interfaith, which they felt intruded on their professional expertise and autonomy in elaborating educational strategies for their students. The community-based organization was construed by teachers to represent an additional demand that was more reflective of administrative directives than their own sense of professional empowerment.

The contrast between Alamo, Palmer, and Sam Houston in regard to the collaboration with Valley Interfaith is striking. At Palmer and Sam Houston, teachers and parents seemed to have acquired an understanding that only their mutual efforts to promote the education of children would generate positive results. Although teachers in both settings expressed minor misgivings about some facets of the work with Valley Interfaith, the overriding impression received by this observer was that Valley Interfaith was viewed by both teachers and parents as a critical ally in the struggle to improve the schools and communities of the Valley. At Alamo, on the other hand, oppositional teachers were outspokenly critical of Valley Interfaith from the very beginning of the initiative. What accounts for the difference in perception by the teachers?

At least part of the difference can probably be attributed to the different organizational structures of secondary schools and elementary schools. When teachers at Palmer conduct home visits to the parents of their students each fall, all of those visits can occur in the scope of a single day. Likewise, when Sam Houston parents hold house meetings in Los Encinos and invite their children's teacher, the restricted size of a class of elementary students allows teachers to meet many parents at once in the intimacy of their homes. The contrast with a secondary school situation is dramatic. At the middle school level—even with the innovative team structure at Alamo—teachers are still conducting instruction for groups of children that range from 90 to 120 each week. Their contact with the students is more fleeting, and the challenge of meeting the parents and forging meaningful ties is greater. Given the scarcity of time for teachers, simply placing the expectation on middle school teachers that they should engage in extensive community outreach is a greater threat for teachers who struggle to preserve a modicum of time not only to plan classes and correct student work but also for personal renewal and the pleasures of a private life.

There are other reasons why the teachers at Alamo might be more resistant to the collaboration with Valley Interfaith. Elementary school teachers are typically more student-centered and secondary school teachers understand themselves as more subject-centered in terms of their orientations to instruction. One can easily see how a teacher who is more focused on helping the whole child to develop than transmitting curricula would find it easier to include the family and the community than a teacher who understands his or her role as the instructor of mathematics or science curricula, strictly delimited. This critical difference in terms of teachers' self-understandings can scarcely be overstated. Alamo teachers were much more explicitly concerned with TAAS results than the elementary school teachers at Palmer and Sam Houston. It is especially noteworthy that their criticisms of the TAAS did not refer to the existence of the test itself, but rather to the standards measured by the TAAS, which they felt were insufficiently rigorous. None of the elementary school teachers at either Palmer or Sam Houston interviewed for this study expressed this concern.

Finally, in terms of the broader context of school change, Deborah Meier has written about the "dearth of experience with progressive education at the secondary level anywhere in the country, even in private or suburban schools that had a tradition of progressive schooling on the elementary level." Secondary schools have a long history of resisting any changes that threaten their organizational structure or a traditional focus on boundaries between disciplines. When one keeps this larger context in mind, the flexibility of Alamo staff in creating the new school team structure should be viewed as a major achievement, and one that in and of itself requires considerable energy in the form of team maintenance and renewal.[14]

It is possible to view the criticisms expressed by Alamo teachers of Valley Interfaith as reflective of a troubled relationship from which little good has emanated. In interviews, Alamo teachers unburdened themselves of their feelings of resentment not only toward the community-based organization, but also toward the school administration that has continued to support the collaborative in the face of outspoken teacher opposition. It would be tempting under these circumstances to view the discord as the manifestation of a relationship that has run its course and should be terminated.

My own view of the matter, however, takes a different tack, for two reasons. First, the mere presence of discord is not necessarily an indication that something inappropriate is occurring. In fact, given the wide body of literature that indicates that teachers are often reluctant to express dissenting opinions toward school administrators, I experienced the open flow of ideas at Alamo as stimulating and a strength of the school culture. From this point of view, Rosi Ruiz's constant readiness to solicit faculty input but at the same time to hold true to her own educational commitments in terms of community engagement indicates strength of leadership in a middle school principal. Likewise, the mere fact that Alamo faculty are continually reflecting upon the nature of their ties to the community and exploring new directions for creating bridging social capital between parents and teachers is, in and of itself, intellectually invigorating, and contributes in a very real way to creation of a stimulating learning community at the school.

Second, even though the change process at Alamo has often been contentious, the school is essentially moving in the right direction in terms of improving student achievement. The rate of progress of sixth and eighth graders on the TAAS surpasses both the district and the state. The seventh grade, by comparison, is progressing more slowly. However, at its current rate of progress, Alamo sixth and eighth graders' scores will surpass both the state and the district in a few years. Thus, it would not appear that this is an appropriate time for any radical changes of course at Alamo.

Certainly, it does seem that some review and clarification of the relationship between Alamo and Valley Interfaith is in order. Alamo teachers and parents do not appear to have developed a house meeting culture, such as that cultivated at Sam Houston, which provides teachers with opportunities for drawing upon parents' cultural resources in enriching instruction. Likewise, Alamo does not appear to be the beneficiary of strong lateral ties to community churches, so it lacks the social capital between school and congregation that Sam Houston draws upon in its relationship with Saint Joseph's the Worker. Perhaps most critically, Alamo teachers do not seem to perceive parents as allies in the struggle to improve their children's education; with a few notable exceptions, the parents are viewed more as obstacles than contributors to student learning. The teachers need opportunities both to express their frustrations in working with parents and to develop new collaborative approaches with the community that will support their mutual interests.

Part of the confusion about the role of Valley Interfaith at Alamo appears to be based on misunderstandings about the nature of the Alliance School initiative. Although Valley Interfaith organizers have led parent- and teacher-training sessions, that is not their primary role; they are not consultants. Likewise, even though Valley Interfaith organizers may assist with school assemblies, school board meetings, or regional Alliance School meetings, those events are not in and of themselves reflective of the purpose of the organizations either. Rather, the purpose of Valley Interfaith is to develop a broad-based organization with sufficient political power to develop indigenous community leaders to act upon their values. This rather inchoate definition reflects a deliberate vagueness on the part of the Industrial Areas Foundation, which continually emphasizes that its work is dependent on agendas set by community members themselves and that modulate over time, depending on the shifting social context. The role of Valley Interfaith thus must be understood as building upon, catalyzing, and deliberately shaping social and cultural processes that have developed over decades through the dynamics of immigration, settlement, schooling, and church participation rather than in starting with the blank slate of an uneducated and apathetic community.

For educators, this philosophical commitment of a community-based group such as Valley Interfaith has real consequences. It indicates that part of the preparation of teachers and administrators must entail learning about the social networks that characterize any given community, and then working carefully and strategically to ensure that the children and parents who make up those networks have opportunities to engage with and enjoy the fruits of the process of schooling. It further entails embracing a social philosophy of education that recognizes that parents have developed their own interpretive schema for making sense of the world—within a given historical and cultural context—and that an important part of the educator's calling is to learn from and engage with parents and other community members. Finally, it suggests the importance of leaving the routines of the classroom and exploring the diversity and intensity of community life—from religious liturgies to cultural festivals to forms of civic leadership—which can provide rich new materials for student engagement and school and community renewal.[15]

The tensions between these new directions implied by the work of a community-based group such as Valley Interfaith and standardized tests such as the TAAS are, of course, tremendous. Valley Interfaith is committed philosophically to reanimating the American tradition of civic engagement, infused with Judeo-Christian values broadly and humanistically construed. The TAAS is a test measuring students' academic skills. To a very real extent, Texas schools that focus only on students' achievement on the TAAS have set themselves a far easier mission than the Alliance Schools. All other things being equal, the tenacious drilling of students for tests generally yields results on those specific instruments. Clearly, one option for educators working in low-income communities is to focus all of their energies on improving student performance on standardized tests. We currently have a number of such schools from around the country in which poor and minority youngsters succeed academically, precisely as a consequence of systematic and often repetitive preparations for standardized tests.

What is wrong with such an approach? On the one hand, it appears defensible on many levels. Youngsters coming from households that are struggling to survive economically succeed in school, and that is no small achievement. Teacher morale improves, and that is also important. The schools receive much favorable press—a particular source of gratification when one is used to the usual litany of criticisms faculty working in public schools receive. In many states principals and teachers now receive bonuses when their students' test results are high. Hence, one can well understand why some educators choose to focus all of their instructional preparation on the standardized tests their students will be taking.

On the other hand, a narrowed focus simply on instruction for standardized test-taking entails a number of troubling consequences. Standardized tests do not measure student achievement in the visual or performing arts, but extensive research indicates that vigorous apprenticeship in these domains, especially at an early age, frequently predicts high achievement across the disciplinary spectrum later on. In their recent book *Teaching the New Basic Skills*, Frank Levy and Richard Murnane argue that "soft" people skills—such as the ability to work collaboratively on teams, accept and give constructive criticism, and problem-solve across a multitude of social settings—is one of the most critical skills demanded by the new information economy, yet this skill also is not measured by the TAAS. The valorizing of certain kinds of knowledge over others—and then reifying them in the contrived manner of standardized tests—entails a host of problems about knowledge construction, student comprehension, and the kinds of skills that our schools and society most value.[16]

Entirely apart from these epistemological problems, there are also political ramifications to a single-minded focus on standardized tests. Jonathan Kozol summarized these in pithy fashion in *Savage Inequalities*. After touring the nation from coast to coast and visiting a multitude of beleaguered inner-city schools, Kozol criticized the apolitical, fragmented nature of orthodox efforts to improve public schooling as follows:

> In many cities, what is termed "restructuring" struck me as very little more than moving around the same old furniture within the house of poverty. The perceived objective was a more "efficient" ghetto school or one with greater "input" from the ghetto parents or more "choices" for the ghetto children. The fact of ghetto education as a permanent American reality appeared to be accepted.[17]

If one substitutes "colonias" for "ghetto" in the above paragraph, one has a clear framing of the issue that confronts educators in the Rio Grande Valley. Is it really acceptable to strive only for high test scores and then to send children back to Las Milpas without any concomitant effort to empower the community? Is it not really imperative for us to address Kozol's critique head-on, and to abolish both "colonias education" and "ghetto education" as a permanent reality?

It might seem paradoxical—and it certainly is ambitious—to seek to combine civic engagement and school reform into a kind of "unified field theory" of educational and community uplift in poor and working-class communities. Yet the case studies presented above, as well as previous scholarship on Alliance Schools, indicate that by bringing hitherto separate realms of social life into fruitful combination one can elicit previously untapped resources for the renewal of schools and communities. For this reason, the development of social capital theory, and particularly the notion of bridging social capital, is of signal importance.

Consider the relationship between religious institutions and public schools. In general, Americans embrace the Jeffersonian and Madisonian legacy, articulated in the Constitution and in many Supreme Court decisions, that a strict wall should separate churches, synagogues, and mosques from the life of public schools. On the one hand, this very separation has strengthened the American body politic by circumscribing the domain of the many particularistic religions that enrich the American civic and cultural landscape. On the other hand, a closer examination of the matter may indicate that we may have been more successful in this regard than is either necessary or productive. In the case of Valley Interfaith, it is worth underlining here that at no point did Saint Joseph's, Resurrection Catholic Church (in Alamo), Saint Margaret's (in Pharr), or Valley Interfaith itself in any way violate the boundary between church and state. In the case studies the notion that churches (and the Catholic Church in particular) do not recognize the separation of church and state is a chimera. Rather, one learns that when fully activated, a church such as Saint Joseph's the Worker can be a crucial asset in the transformation and blossoming of a public school such as Sam Houston Elementary. Previous research on Alliance Schools indicates that the same claims can be made about churches collaborating with schools that serve predominantly African American populations.[18]

One lesson that might be taken from the Alliance School experiment—not just in South Texas but throughout the state network—is that the separation of church and state is, in point of fact, not just a peripheral issue to this kind of school reform but a powerful conceptual barrier to developing bridging social capital in poor and working-class communities. Faith-based institutions and schools have common interests in healthy children, strong families, and safe and prosperous communities. Given the wealth of scholarship that indicates that membership in religious institutions is a powerful social asset, particularly for poor and working-class children, the new interest in faith-based institutions as resources for the young represents a significant advance over their previous marginality or even invisibility in matters of educational policy.[19]

In the current political context for American schools, in which vouchers, for-profit schools, and privatization dominate headlines, it is worth underlining that we are considering horizontal ties between religious institutions, community organizations, and schools not as strategies for *subverting* strong public schools but as means of *strengthening* and improving them. For this observer, as for most Americans, it is self-evident that a free and democratic polity should embrace a plurality of school forms, including the Catholic, Protestant, Jewish, and nondenominational schools that enrich the American pedagogical mosaic. It is far less obvious that religious institutions can play a valuable role in promoting strong public schools; hence the significance of the Alliance Schools as a challenge to mainstream understandings.

Even as a rapprochement might be effected between public schools and religious institutions—unified through a joint commitment to youths and their families—it would be erroneous to indicate that a congregationally based approach to community organizing for school reform could provide anything approaching a total solution to the problems of contemporary American schools. Although the people of the United States are unusually devout in comparison with those of other industrialized nations, a significant minority—43 percent—do not see themselves as affiliated with any religious institution. Roughly three quarters of Hispanic Catholics are not practicing, and research indicates that those who do participate have important criticisms of the Church and would especially like to see a greater representation of Hispanics in positions of leadership. Furthermore, religious institutions and community-based organizations are important primarily in changing the *context* of education. However much their influence might be felt in changing the climate toward learning in a community, such influence is unlikely to have any lasting impact unless it is accompanied by parallel work, both inside and outside schools, that develops more powerful forms of learning by students.[20]

Yet even given those caveats, the linkages that can be formed between schools, congregations, and community organizations clearly can produce powerful networks that sustain children's academic achievement. Even if three-fourths of Hispanic Catholics are unchurched, the obverse side of that coin indicates that one-fourth do attend church, where they observe Mass, serve on parish councils, attend Bible study groups, and in general further both their spiritual growth and social networks with one another. Even if a large minority of Americans do not participate in the lives of religious institutions, a majority are actively involved, and those social networks represent a powerful resource for public schools and their communities.

The evidence presented above suggests that the boundary between church and state is well respected by the Alliance School initiative, even when evidence is available of a visible connectedness that promotes social capitalization between congregations and schools. Can the same be said about respecting the boundary between politics and schools?

It is not clear that the same claim can be advanced about a disinterested political neutrality in the work of the Alliance Schools. As the case of Alamo Middle School revealed, some teachers felt urged by members of the school administration to support the political agenda of Valley Interfaith. Those oppositional teachers felt that the administration had no business exhorting them to support anyone's agenda, regardless of the nonpartisan nature of Valley Interfaith's activities or the effort to build a broad base of community support for desperately needed infrastructural improvements in the colonias. For those teachers, the administration's appeals reinforced their initial reservations about collaborating with Valley Interfaith and suggested that although the community organization claimed to be offering first and foremost a strategy for parental engagement, subsequent developments led it to seek a more ambitious and perhaps self-interested position in the school's culture. Clearly, if collaborative efforts by schools and community organizations are to be successful—if bridging social capital is to be built between schools and *political* associations like Valley Interfaith—greater clarification of the nature of those relationships will be of critical importance.

Given the contested situation at Alamo, it is striking that interviews with teachers and parents at Palmer and Sam Houston indicated minimal tension between the politics of Valley Interfaith and their schools. Yet it may be that more is at work here than initially meets the eye. Both Palmer and Sam Houston appear to have concentrated much energy on developing *bridging* forms of social capital that link the school through strong interpersonal relationships with community leaders in Las Milpas and Saint Joseph's the Worker, respectively. Alamo Middle School, on the other hand, focused primarily on the internal consolidation of the school—on the arena that social scientists call *bonding* social capital of individuals within an institution. That emphasis has had an important consequence: on the whole, the social networks between Alamo faculty, students' parents, and Valley Interfaith appear to be weaker than in Palmer and Sam Houston. The fragility of those ties has thus brought the collaborative under critical scrutiny, and more attention has been given to its formal conditions than might occur in situations where partners such as Sister Maria and Connie Maheshwari (in McAllen) or Salvador Flores and Carmen Anaya (in Pharr) have longstanding friendships with one another.

It is, of course, in the inherent nature of social relationships that misunderstandings and conflict occur. When Valley Interfaith organizers were queried about the stance of oppositional teachers at Alamo, they were cautious and said that any implication that teachers needed to support their agenda as part of their professional roles was erroneous. In addition, many of the relationships that worked well in the Alliance Schools described above could sour in other settings. Connie Maheshwari, for example, recognized that it is "possible for parental involvement to get out of hand, and one day you wake up and find that you've created a monster." She herself has had problems with parents who have disrespected the autonomy of her teachers and herself and have created difficulties for Sam Houston. "Part of the issue is that parents have never had a chance to come at you before, so that when you first try to bring them in, there is a tendency for them to want to go after you. But I try to see that there is a part of that that is good. It's good for them to ask hard questions. And it's my job to make sure that I've got some good answers for whatever it is that is bothering them." In other words, the parental-engagement process, like that of the larger process of community collaboration, is developmental. Any expectations that the process will be without either friction or a need for clarification and reconceptualization are likely to be disappointed.[21]

None of this suggests that efforts to increase parental engagement and to develop schools into centers of community life should be constrained. These reflections about new kinds of collaborations between community organizations, public schools, and religious institutions are part of an exciting debate among Americans that is appropriately placing issues of civil society—issues concerning our families, secondary associations, and cultural life—at the heart of the national agenda. It is at this juncture that the work of the Alliance Schools in South Texas possesses meaning not just for their immediate region, nor simply for Mexican Americans or Mexican immigrants, but for the nation as a whole. For while residents of the Rio Grande Valley may struggle with seemingly intractable problems related to education, health care, and low-wage employment, it is hardly the case that mainstream American society is immune to these problems. It is increasingly evident that a host of developments—including globalization, technological change, the increasing uncertainty of stable long-term employment, and declining social capital—have created precarious conditions for the nurturance of America's youths and families.

In this context, learning about innovative strategies for school reform and community betterment carried out in one of the nation's poorest and most disadvantaged regions carries important lessons. For if it is possible to develop new kinds of school reform that are linked to community life and overcome hitherto obdurate boundaries that have isolated communities, congregations, and schools from one another in the Rio Grande Valley, it would also seem to hold that similar innovations might be explored elsewhere that may offer new possibilities for a richer civic and educational life than have previously been available to many communities.

Certainly, it is important to recognize the problems that the three Alliance Schools described above are confronting in their work. The major difficulty faced by each of the campuses is that its parental-engagement strategy has not translated directly into gains in student academic achievement. Palmer's TAAS scores have generally improved at a rate lower than the state and district; Alamo has made impressive gains at the sixth and eighth grade levels, but not at the seventh; Sam Houston reached exemplary status on the TAAS in 1998 but experienced slippage the following year. Social capitalization, in the form of the kind of parental engagement advocated by Valley Interfaith, would seem to be an uncertain predictor of student achievement on standardized tests like the TAAS.

In addition to the indirect outcomes of parental engagement for the TAAS, this study has documented hidden costs of these attempts to cultivate social capital, in the most dramatic form through oppositional teachers at Alamo. Teachers resented the intensification of their work through the collaboration with Valley Interfaith; they disliked administrators who urged them to support Valley Interfaith's strategies and made inroads on their professional autonomy; and they wanted to preserve as much time as possible to focus their energies on classroom instruction. It appears that school reformers who seek to use social capital as a theoretical tool to advance their work should continue to do so, but only by reckoning directly with these hidden costs and developing strategies to address teachers' real concerns.

In spite of the problems with the TAAS, or with the parental-engagement strategy at Alamo, or with the persistence of poverty in the Rio Grande Valley, I hope that readers of this volume have gained the impression that all three of the schools are fascinating institutions engaged in the most important of struggles. Palmer, Alamo, and Sam Houston are schools that are willing to take risks, committed to improving the education of the children in their charge, and very much aware of the changing economic and political context that their children will confront in the new century. To be sure, work that links community and school improvement simultaneously is relatively new and untested, and although the initial findings are intriguing, much further experimentation is needed to assess the merits of the new strategies. Through this undertaking a crucial lesson might be learned, which could indicate that public schools can indeed evolve into the vibrant centers of civic activism and academic achievement we all would like them to be—if we are willing to engage in the difficult work of reconceptualizing and renewing the relationships between schools, households, and secondary associations that can support and educate our children.

APPENDIX

The appendix presents TAAS data for the three schools in summary form. Readers who would like additional information on the schools are advised to consult the voluminous data compiled by the Texas Education Agency on the website of its Academic Excellence Indicator System at www.tea.state.tx.us/perfreport/aeis/index.html. This site provides not only TAAS outcomes for every school in Texas but also information on school attendance rates, graduation rates (for high schools), and percentages of students in each school who are in special education or ESL programs. The one major limitation of the listings on the site is that only the percentages of students passing the different sections of the TAAS are listed—not the number of test takers. Those numbers can only be acquired by contacting the school, the school district, or administrators at either the Communication Division or the Student Assessment Division of the Texas Education Agency. As the analysis in the text indicates, the low numbers of students taking different sections of the TAAS in the two elementary schools must be kept in mind when attempting to gauge improvements in student learning.

TABLE I Reading, Math, and Writing[+] TAAS scores for Palmer Elementary School, 1996–1999

	Texas		Pharr–San Juan–Alamo Independent School District		Palmer Elementary		Economically Disadvantaged (Palmer)		Economically Disadvantaged (Texas)	
GRADE 3										
Reading										
1999	88.0%	(232,984)	88.4%	(1,162)	84.4%	(51)	81.6%	(49)	81.6%	(110,716)
1998	86.2%	(223,856)	91.0%	(1,036)	82.2%	(49)	78.8%	(48)	79.0%	(106,049)
1997	81.5%	(219,521)	84.5%	(954)	82.9%	(38)	73.9%	(36)	72.0%	(102,964)
1996	80.5%	(215,655)	82.9%	(923)	81.5%	(30)	76.2%	(27)	70.1%	(99,950)
Math										
1999	83.1%	(234,160)	85.6%	(995)	76.6%	(51)	77.5%	(49)	75.1%	(111,645)
1998	81.0%	(224,910)	86.9%	(957)	75.6%	(49)	72.7%	(48)	72.2%	(106,871)
1997	81.7%	(220,278)	87.2%	(1,033)	83.3%	(38)	75.0%	(36)	73.3%	(103,531)
1996	76.7%	(215,896)	86.8%	(928)	96.3%	(30)	95.2%	(27)	66.4%	(100,148)
GRADE 4										
Reading										
1999	88.8%	(231,100)	89.9%	(1,184)	88.9%	(60)	85.0%	(55)	82.3%	(108,434)
1998	89.7%	(224,291)	93.7%	(1,014)	95.3%	(48)	93.5%	(47)	83.4%	(104,354)
1997	82.5%	(221,875)	83.6%	(1,063)	90.9%	(34)	90.9%	(34)	73.0%	(102,504)
1996	78.3%	(213,616)	76.6%	(1,152)	78.8%	(35)	78.8%	(35)	67.5%	(97,608)

Math					
1999	87.6% (232,035)	91.2% (1,204)	91.5% (60)	88.9% (55)	81.3% (109,255)
1998	86.3% (224,930)	89.6% (1,165)	88.1% (48)	83.3% (47)	79.5% (104,875)
1997	82.6% (222,095)	87.5% (1,011)	93.9% (34)	93.9% (34)	73.9% (102,803)
1996	78.5% (213,580)	82.9% (1,052)	81.8% (35)	81.8% (35)	68.3% (97,607)
Writing					
1999	88.4% (240,462)	91.0% (1,159)	85.2% (60)	80.5% (55)	83.3% (87,919)
1998	88.7% (242,811)	93.1% (999)	95.3% (48)	92.5% (47)	83.0% (91,733)
1997	87.1% (239,319)	89.0% N/A	97.1% (34)	97.1% (34)	80.4% (91,690)
1996	86.3% (218,164)	89.1% (992)	96.4% (35)	96.4% (35)	79.9% (100,129)
GRADE 5					
Reading					
1999	86.4% (234,913)	84.9% (1,150)	75.0% (46)	66.7% (43)	78.0% (109,183)
1998	88.4% (229,083)	92.2% (1,132)	97.1% (36)	97.1% (36)	81.7% (105,412)
1997	84.8% (229,488)	79.7% (1,174)	69.8% (45)	64.9% (44)	75.7% (105,429)
1996	83.0% (229,085)	84.0% (1,130)	67.4% (49)	64.3% (48)	73.1% (102,829)
Math					
1999	90.1% (235,149)	94.6% (1,171)	92.9% (46)	90.3% (43)	84.9% (109,461)
1998	89.6% (229,414)	95.1% (1,418)	97.1% (36)	97.1% (36)	84.0% (105,705)
1997	86.2% (229,607)	88.7% (1,130)	75.6% (45)	74.3% (44)	78.7% (105,627)
1996	79.0% (228,980)	87.6% (1,157)	67.4% (49)	64.3% (48)	68.7% (102,804)

*Writing Scores for Grade 4 Only

(Numbers in parentheses represent total number of students taking the TAAS)

TABLE 2 Spanish-Language Reading and Math Scores, Palmer Elementary School, 1997–1999

	Texas	Pharr–San Juan–Alamo Independent School District	Palmer Elementary	Economically Disadvantaged (Palmer)	Economically Disadvantaged (Texas)
SPANISH GRADE 3					
Reading					
1999	74.2% (17,280)	63.7% (159)	64.3% (14)	64.3% (14)	73.8% (14,031)
1998	65.6% (19,110)	52.7% (358)	36.8% (20)	36.8% (20)	65.4% (16,029)
1997	44.6% (18,552)	37.0% (448)	47.4% (22)	47.4% (22)	44.3% (15,897)
Math					
1999	74.9% (17,186)	62.7% (155)	78.6% (14)	78.6% (14)	74.6% (15,409)
1998	65.0% (18,433)	60.8% (337)	47.4% (20)	47.4% (20)	66.3% (16,029)
1997	53.5% (18,535)	47.5% (449)	50.0% (22)	50.0% (22)	53.2% (15,897)
SPANISH GRADE 4					
Reading					
1999	46.1% (10,897)	55.2% (70)	50.0% (16)	50.0% (16)	45.4% (8,659)
1998	38.6% (13,188)	29.8% (325)	58.3% (14)	58.3% (14)	38.6% (11,286)
1997	36.8% (12,192)	30.1% (273)	30.8% (16)	30.8% (16)	36.5% (10,544)

Math									
1999	72.7%	(10,315)	78.0%	(69)	91.7%	(16)	91.7%	(16)	72.3%	(9,351)
1998	58.3%	(13,056)	49.1%	(312)	58.3%	(14)	66.7%	(14)	58.3%	(11,286)
1997	48.0%	(12,217)	45.8%	(274)	51.8%	(16)	38.5%	(16)	46.0%	(10,544)

SPANISH GRADE 5

Reading									
1999	33.5%	(6,605)	29.1%	(163)	14.3%	(12)	14.3%	(12)	32.8%	(5,203)
1998	49.0%	(7,781)	38.2%	(213)	42.9%	(14)	38.5%	(13)	48.9%	(6,586)
Math									
1999	65.1%	(6,221)	63.8%	(160)	50.0%	(12)	50.0%	(12)	64.5%	(5,716)
1998	56.5%	(7,716)	50.6%	(199)	57.1%	(14)	53.8%	(13)	56.7%	(6,586)

(Numbers in parentheses represent total number of students taking the TAAS)

TABLE 3   Percentages of Students Passing the Reading, Math, and Writing[+] Sections of the TAAS, Alamo Middle School, 1993–1999

	Texas	Pharr–San Juan–Alamo Independent School District	Alamo Middle	Economically Disadvantaged (Alamo)	Economically Disadvantaged (Texas)
GRADE 6					
Reading					
1999	84.9% (261,704)	79.4% (1,275)	80.8% (241)	79.9% (201)	76.1% (94,821)
1998	85.6% (267,044)	71.9% (1,239)	75.7% (239)	73.3% (158)	75.8% (100,821)
1997	84.6% (266,694)	70.9% (1,225)	73.9% (233)	71.9% (191)	74.3% (100,326)
1996	78.4% (233,048)	55.9% (1,176)	59.8% (247)	58.6% (219)	64.6% (103,406)
1995	78.9% (232,527)	65.7% (1,210)	63.6% (247)	59.7% (213)	66.7% (98,574)
1994	74.1% (232,312)	61.5% (1,203)	55.6% (255)	51.0% (219)	60.1% (96,262)
Math					
1999	86.9% (263,847)	89.0% (1,278)	89.1% (241)	89.2% (201)	80.2% (96,200)
1998	86.1% (268,503)	83.3% (1,235)	82.7% (239)	81.7% (158)	78.4% (101,684)
1997	81.8% (267,428)	77.3% (1,231)	78.0% (233)	76.3% (191)	71.7% (100,808)
1996	77.8% (232,802)	66.5% (1,175)	75.7% (247)	76.1% (219)	66.1% (103,235)
1995	64.6% (232,350)	51.0% (1,215)	43.2% (247)	37.6% (213)	48.6% (98,488)
1994	61.1% (232,840)	55.2% (1,193)	41.8% (255)	39.4% (216)	45.4% (96,500)
GRADE 7					
Reading					
1999	83.6% (265,852)	72.6% (1,257)	73.2% (244)	70.4% (202)	73.6% (90,248)
1998	85.5% (271,011)	73.2% (1,252)	76.2% (243)	74.9% (178)	75.5% (94,685)

1997	84.5% (263,534)	65.5% (1,229)	69.3% (248)	68.8% (203)	74.0% (93,424)
1996	82.6% (237,154)	67.6% (1,233)	65.5% (266)	62.4% (238)	71.4% (97,391)
1995	78.7% (234,670)	64.6% (1,190)	64.2% (250)	61.2% (213)	65.9% (91,974)
1994	75.9% (230,131)	61.0% (1,210)	66.3% (208)	62.5% (174)	61.0% (86,845)
Math					
1999	84.9% (266,437)	80.5% (1,250)	77.4% (244)	75.2% (202)	77.0% (90,758)
1998	83.7% (271,295)	78.9% (1,249)	80.3% (243)	79.3% (178)	73.7% (94,979)
1997	79.7% (263,350)	71.8% (1,227)	75.6% (248)	74.6% (203)	68.8% (93,395)
1996	71.5% (236,631)	60.6% (1,236)	61.9% (266)	58.8% (238)	56.6% (97,106)
1995	62.3% (234,496)	47.7% (1,193)	45.8% (250)	43.3% (211)	44.5% (91,922)
1994	59.7% (230,645)	43.8% (1,211)	47.5% (208)	44.4% (173)	42.2% (87,071)
GRADE 8					
Reading					
1999	88.2% (263,656)	79.7% (1,256)	85.7% (238)	84.1% (187)	80.7% (81,846)
1998	85.3% (262,890)	69.0% (1,282)	74.0% (248)	71.6% (203)	74.8% (156,248)
1997	83.9% (259,351)	69.0% (1,284)	73.6% (248)	70.4% (203)	72.7% (84,471)
1996	78.3% (233,348)	64.7% (1,212)	64.3% (248)	60.5% (230)	64.3% (88,833)
1995	75.5% (227,384)	61.9% (1,165)	62.8% (248)	58.4% (183)	60.5% (81,321)
1994	77.2% (222,588)	61.0% (1,180)	68.5% (229)	65.5% (191)	61.9% (77,479)
1993	71.8% N/A	46.0% N/A	53.3% (229)	47.0% N/A	53.4% N/A

TABLE 3 Continued

	Texas		Pharr–San Juan–Alamo Independent School District		Alamo Middle		Economically Disadvantaged (Alamo)		Economically Disadvantaged (Texas)	
Math										
1999	86.3%	(263,164)	84.3%	(1,253)	88.6%	(238)	89.3%	(187)	78.7%	(81,842)
1998	83.8%	(262,319)	77.2%	(1,277)	79.8%	(248)	78.7%	(203)	74.6%	(86,430)
1997	76.3%	(259,059)	67.0%	(1,281)	70.8%	(248)	68.1%	(203)	63.6%	(84,367)
1996	69.0%	(232,786)	58.8%	(1,214)	56.9%	(248)	55.1%	(230)	53.4%	(88,644)
1995	57.3%	(227,133)	39.3%	(1,185)	33.7%	(248)	31.3%	(184)	37.8%	(81,260)
1994	58.6%	(223,061)	42.1%	(1,182)	47.7%	(229)	45.9%	(188)	39.9%	(77,837)
1993	51.1%	N/A	26.5%	N/A	30.1%	(229)	25.5%	N/A	30.1%	N/A
Writing										
1999	85.7%	(259,045)	83.1%	(1,231)	88.9%	N/A	87.1%	N/A	77.6%	(80,821)
1998	84.0%	(259,787)	74.8%	(1,240)	84.1%	N/A	82.6%	N/A	74.7%	(85,952)
1997	80.7%	(256,214)	70.5%	(1,277)	73.5%	N/A	70.4%	N/A	69.4%	(83,986)
1996	76.9%	(231,464)	67.6%	(1,252)	67.5%	(254)	66.2%	(217)	63.8%	(88,848)
1995	75.3%	(225,215)	59.9%	(1,251)	63.3%	(224)	60.8%	(192)	62.2%	(81,436)
1994	69.8%	(224,852)	59.7%	(1,228)	62.9%	(234)	59.1%	(205)	55.0%	(79,568)
1993	73.9%	N/A	60.5%	N/A	67.1%	N/A	63.1%	N/A	58.9%	N/A

+Writing Scores for Grade 8 Only
(Numbers in parentheses represent total number of students taking the TAAS)

TABLE 4 Percentages of Sixth-Grade Students Passing the Spanish-Language TAAS in Reading and Math, Alamo Middle School, 1998–1999

	Texas	Pharr–San Juan–Alamo Independent School District	Alamo Middle	Economically Disadvantaged (Alamo)	Economically Disadvantaged (Texas)
SPANISH GRADE 6					
Reading					
1999	30.2% (1,686)	*% N/A (19)	*% N/A (19)	*% N/A (18)	30.2% (1,226)
1998	28.2% (1,872)	37.2% (19)	37.0% (19)	37.5% (18)	28.0% (1,496)
Math					
1999	51.2% (1,651)	*% N/A (20)	*% N/A (20)	*% N/A (19)	52.1% (1,420)
1998	38.2% (1,845)	30.0% (20)	30.0% (20)	29.4% (19)	38.4% (1,496)

* data unavailable at time of publishing
(Numbers in parentheses represent total number of students taking the TAAS)

TABLE 5 Percentages of Students Passing the Reading, Math, and Writing⁺ Sections of the TAAS, Sam Houston Elementary School, 1993–1999

	Texas	McAllen Independent School District	Sam Houston Elementary	Economically Disadvantaged (S.H.)	Economically Disadvantaged (Texas)
GRADE 3					
Reading					
1999	88.0% (232,984)	89.0% (1,311)	82.8% (67)	80.7% (60)	81.6% (110,716)
1998	86.2% (223,856)	83.3% (1,356)	100.0% (42)	100.0% (38)	79.0% (106,049)
1997	81.5% (219,521)	75.0% (1,419)	80.0% (47)	78.0% (43)	72.0% (102,964)
1996	80.5% (215,655)	80.8% (1,084)	77.8% (46)	76.5% (43)	70.1% (99,950)
1995	79.5% (216,749)	78.2% (1,194)	58.3% (37)	59.4% (33)	68.7% (97,876)
1994	77.9% (222,005)	83.3% (1,157)	91.5% (48)	90.2% (42)	66.4% (97,811)
Math					
1999	83.1% (234,160)	84.4% (1,336)	87.7% (67)	86.2% (60)	75.1% (111,645)
1998	81.0% (224,910)	78.3% (1,363)	92.3% (42)	91.4% (38)	72.2% (106,871)
1997	81.7% (220,278)	79.5% (1,411)	82.2% (47)	80.5% (43)	73.3% (103,351)
1996	76.7% (215,896)	78.6% (1,078)	77.8% (46)	76.5% (43)	66.4% (100,148)
1995	73.3% (217,114)	69.8% (1,196)	35.1% (39)	36.4% (35)	61.8% (98,126)
1994	63.0% (222,905)	62.0% (1,155)	85.1% (48)	85.4% (42)	49.1% (98,387)

GRADE 4

Reading

Year					
1999	88.8% (231,100)	91.5% (1,333)	96.0% [51]	95.2% (43)	82.3% (108,434)
1998	89.7% (224,291)	89.7% (1,398)	96.2% [52]	96.0% (50)	83.4% (104,354)
1997	82.5% (221,875)	84.3% (1,361)	86.7% [53]	86.0% (51)	73.0% (102,504)
1996	78.3% (213,616)	82.9% (1,138)	82.9% [37]	84.4% (34)	67.5% (97,608)
1995	80.1% (222,716)	86.8% (1,201)	95.1% [42]	94.3% (36)	69.2% (98,623)
1994	75.5% (219,390)	82.5% (1,158)	69.0% [45]	68.3% (43)	63.3% (96,949)
1993	65.5% N/A	69.8% N/A	64.3% N/A	63.4% N/A	49.4% N/A

Math

Year					
1999	87.6% (232,035)	91.4% (1,367)	98.1% [52]	97.7% (43)	81.3% (109,255)
1998	86.3% (224,930)	88.9% (1,414)	84.6% [52]	84.0% (50)	79.5% (104,875)
1997	82.6% (222,095)	85.8% (1,358)	88.9% [53]	90.7% (51)	73.9% (102,803)
1996	78.5% (213,580)	81.9% (1,142)	82.9% [37]	84.4% (34)	68.3% (97,607)
1995	71.1% (222,874)	74.1% (1,201)	85.4% [42]	82.9% (36)	58.2% (98,723)
1994	59.4% (220,151)	66.6% (1,163)	66.7% [45]	65.9% (43)	45.7% (97,383)
1993	52.6% N/A	52.9% N/A	54.8% N/A	53.7% N/A	36.9% N/A

Writing

Year					
1999	88.4% (240,462)	90.3% (1,267)	88.0% [51]	90.2% (42)	83.3% (87,919)
1998	88.7% (242,811)	88.5% (1,235)	90.4% [52]	90.0% (50)	83.0% (91,733)
1997	87.1% (239,319)	86.6% N/A	91.1% [55]	90.7% (53)	80.4% (91,690)
1996	86.3% (218,164)	88.0% (1,142)	80.0% [36]	78.1% (33)	79.9% (100,129)
1995	85.0% (219,057)	88.8% (1,165)	97.6% [42]	97.1% (36)	77.2% (97,267)
1994	85.5% (219,860)	91.3% (1,167)	85.0% [43]	84.6% (41)	77.4% (97,937)
1993	83.4% N/A	88.0% N/A	86.0% N/A	85.7% N/A	73.8% N/A

TABLE 5 Continued

	Texas		McAllen Independent School District		Sam Houston Elementary		Economically Disadvantaged (S.H.)		Economically Disadvantaged (Texas)	
GRADE 5										
Reading										
1999	86.4%	(234,913)	87.8%	(1,308)	80.4%	(55)	78.8%	(51)	78.0%	(109,183)
1998	88.4%	(229,083)	91.5%	(1,342)	100.0%	(51)	100.0%	(49)	81.7%	(105,412)
1997	84.8%	(229,488)	87.7%	(1,472)	92.5%	(43)	92.3%	(42)	75.7%	(105,429)
1996	83.0%	(229,085)	89.3%	(1,223)	85.4%	(44)	83.8%	(30)	73.1%	(102,829)
1995	79.3%	(223,588)	84.7%	(1,250)	86.0%	(46)	85.7%	(45)	68.4%	(98,954)
1994	77.5%	(225,487)	86.4%	(1,225)	88.6%	(50)	88.4%	(49)	65.4%	(97,857)
Math										
1999	90.1%	(235,149)	92.7%	(1,325)	89.1%	(54)	88.2%	(50)	84.9%	(109,461)
1998	89.6%	(229,414)	93.3%	(1,345)	96.0%	(51)	97.9%	(49)	84.0%	(105,705)
1997	86.2%	(229,607)	90.6%	(1,466)	89.7%	(42)	89.5%	(41)	78.7%	(105,627)
1996	79.0%	(228,980)	88.3%	(1,225)	92.7%	(44)	91.9%	(40)	68.7%	(102,804)
1995	72.6%	(223,531)	78.1%	(1,256)	88.6%	(47)	88.4%	(46)	60.2%	(98,964)
1994	62.6%	(226,058)	73.3%	(1,226)	58.1%	(49)	57.1%	(48)	48.4%	(98,174)

[+]Writing Scores for Grade 4 Only
(Numbers in parentheses represent total number of students taking the TAAS)

TABLE 6 Percentages of Third-Grade Students Passing Spanish-Language Administrations of the TAAS in Reading and Math, Sam Houston Elementary School, 1997–1999

	Texas		McAllen Independent School District		Sam Houston Elementary		Economically Disadvantaged (S.H.)		Economically Disadvantaged (Texas)	
SPANISH GRADE 3										
Reading										
1999	74.2%	(17,280)	88.9%	(29)	84.0%	(67)	82.0%	(60)	73.8%	(14,031)
1998	65.6%	(19,110)	50.0%	(79)	23.5%	N/A	23.5%	N/A	65.4%	(16,029)
1997	44.6%	(18,552)	38.1%	(56)	23.1%	(13)	23.1%	(13)	44.3%	(15,897)
Math										
1999	74.9%	(16,678)	90.0%	(22)	*%	N/A	*%	N/A	74.6%	(15,559)
1998	66.4%	(18,920)	53.1%	(69)	23.5%	N/A	23.5%	N/A	66.3%	(16,029)
1997	53.5%	(18,535)	40.5%	(56)	23.1%	(13)	23.1%	(13)	53.2%	(15,897)

* data unavailable at time of publishing
(Numbers in parentheses represent total number of students taking the TAAS)

NOTES

INTRODUCTION

1. Numerous recent studies have focused upon Mexican-origin Americans and recent Mexican immigration to the United States. The major works I have consulted include David Montejano, *Anglos and Mexicans in the Making of Texas, 1836–1986* (Austin: University of Texas, 1987); Mario T. García, *Mexican Americans: Leadership, Ideology, and Identity, 1930–1960* (New Haven: Yale University Press, 1989); Lawrence A. Herzog, *Where North Meets South: Cities, Space, and Politics on the U.S.-Mexico Border* (Austin: University of Texas Press, 1990); John R. Weeks and Roberto Ham-Chande, eds., *Demographic Dynamics of the U.S.-Mexico Border* (El Paso: Texas Western Press, 1992); Américo Paredes, *Folklore and Culture on the Texas-Mexican Border* (Austin: Center for Mexican American Studies, 1993); Peter Skerry, *Mexican Americans: The Ambivalent Minority* (New York: Free Press, 1993); Pierette Hondagenu-Sotelo, *Gendered Transitions: Mexican Experiences of Immigration* (Berkeley: University of California Press, 1994); Roberto M. De Anda, ed., *Chicanas and Chicanos in Contemporary Society* (Boston: Allyn and Bacon, 1996); David G. Gutiérrez, ed., *Between Two Worlds: Mexican Immigrants in the United States* (Wilmington, Del.: Scholarly Resources, 1996); Carlos G. Vélez-Ibáñez, *Border Visions: Mexican Cultures of the Southwest United States* (Tucson: University of Arizona Press, 1996); Frank D. Bean et al., *At the Crossroads: Mexico and U.S. Immigration Policy* (Lanham, Md.: Rowman and Littlefield, 1997); Marcelo M. Suárez-Orozco, ed., *Crossings: Mexican Immigration in Interdisciplinary Perspectives* (Cambridge: Harvard University Press, 1998); Roberto Suro, *Strangers among Us: How Latino Immigration Is Transforming America* (New York: Knopf, 1998).

2. Recent contributions on Mexican Americans and academic achievement include Concha Delgado-Gaitan, *Literacy for Empower-*

ment: *The Role of Parents in Children's Education* (Philadelphia: Falmer, 1990); Richard R. Valencia, ed., *Chicano School Failure and Success: Research and Policy Agendas for the 1990s* (Philadelphia: Falmer, 1991); Olga A. Vasquez, Lucinda Pease-Alvarez, and Sheila M. Shannon, *Pushing Boundaries: Language and Culture in a Mexicano Community* (Cambridge: Cambridge University Press, 1994); Carola Suárez-Orozco and Marcelo Suárez-Orozco, *Transformations: Immigration, Family Life, and Achievement Motivation among Latino Adolescents* (Stanford: Stanford University Press, 1995); Harriett D. Romo and Toni Falbo, *Latino High School Graduation: Defying the Odds* (Austin: University of Texas Press, 1996); Guadalupe Valdés, *Con Respeto: Bridging the Distances between Culturally Diverse Families and Schools* (New York: Teachers College Press, 1996); Enrique Trueba, "The Education of Mexican Immigrant Children," in *Crossings*, 251–75; Marleen C. Pugach, *On the Border of Opportunity: Education, Community, and Language at the U.S.-Mexico Line* (Mahwah, N.J.: Lawrence Erlbaum, 1998); Guadalupe San Miguel Jr. and Richard R. Valencia, "From the Treaty of Guadalupe Hidalgo to *Hopwood:* The Educational Plight and Struggle of Mexican Americans in the Southwest," *Harvard Educational Review* 68, no. 3 (1998): 353–412; José F. Moreno, ed., *The Elusive Quest for Equality: 150 Years of Chicano/Chicana Education* (Cambridge: Harvard Educational Review, 1999); Angela Valenzuela, *Subtractive Schooling: U.S.-Mexican Youth and the Politics of Caring* (Albany: State University of New York Press, 1999).

3. Dennis Shirley, *Community Organizing for Urban School Reform* (Austin: University of Texas Press, 1997). See also Mary E. Driscoll, "Thinking like a Fish: The Implications of the Image of School Community for Connections between Parents and Schools," in *Transforming Schools,* ed. Peter W. Cookson Jr. and Barbara Schneider (New York: Garland Publishing, 1995), 209–36; James G. Cibulka, "Conclusion: Toward an Interpretation of School, Family, and Community Connections: Policy Challenges," in *Coordination among Schools, Families, and Communities: Prospects for Educational Reform,* ed. James G. Cibulka and William J. Kritek (Albany: State University of New York Press, 1996), 403–35; Gene I. Maeroff, "Altered Destinies: Making Life Better for Schoolchildren in Need," *Phi Delta Kappan* 79, no. 6 (Feb. 1998): 425–32.

4. On Americans' falling confidence in public schools, see Jean Johnson et al., *Assignment Incomplete: The Unfinished Business of Education Reform* (New York: Public Agenda, 1995), 13. On the growing division between the rich and poor in the United States and declining levels of civic engagement, see Robert D. Putnam, *Bowling Alone: The Collapse and Revival of American Community* (New York: Simon and

Schuster, 2000); Jean Bethke Elshtain, *Democracy on Trial* (New York: Basic, 1995); Keith Bradsher, "Gap in Wealth in U.S. Called Widest in West," *New York Times,* 17 Apr. 1995, and "Low Ranking for Poor American Children: U.S. Youth among Worst Off in Study of 18 Industrialized Nations," *New York Times,* 14 Aug. 1995; David C. Johnson, "Gap between Rich and Poor Found Substantially Wider," *New York Times,* 5 Sept. 1999; Theda Skocpol and Richard C. Leone, *The Missing Middle: Working Families and the Future of American Social Policy* (New York: W. W. Norton, 2000).

5. On the transformation of American public education through the use of standardized tests, see George F. Madaus, "The Influence of Testing on the Curriculum," in *Critical Issues in Curriculum,* ed. Laurel N. Tanner (Chicago: University of Chicago Press, 1988), 83–121; National Commission on Testing and Public Policy, *From Gatekeeper to Gateway: Transforming Testing in America* (Chestnut Hill, Mass.: National Commission on Testing and Public Policy, 1990); Walter M. Haney, George F. Madaus, and Robert Lyons, *The Fractured Marketplace for Standardized Testing* (Boston: Kluwer Academic Publishers, 1993); George F. Madaus, "A Technological and Historical Consideration of Equity Issues Associated with Proposals to Change the Nation's Testing Policy," *Harvard Educational Review* 64, no. 1 (spring 1994): 76–95. On the impact of changing testing practices on instruction in Texas, see Linda McNeil, *Contradictions of School Reform: Educational Costs of Standardized Testing* (New York: Routledge, 2000), and Debra Viadero, "Testing System in Texas Yet to Get Final Grade," *Education Week,* 31 May 2000.

6. Walter M. Haney, "Testing and Minorities," in *Beyond Silenced Voices: Class, Race, and Gender in United States Schools,* ed. Lois Weis and Michelle Fine (Albany: State University of New York Press, 1993), 45–73; quotes from 71–73. For a recent summary of the debate about testing in Texas, see Viadero, "Testing System in Texas," 1.

7. Gary S. Becker revolutionized the economics of education a generation ago in his *Human Capital: A Theoretical and Empirical Analysis, with Special Reference to Education* (New York: National Bureau of Economic Research, 1964).

8. Glenn Loury, "A Dynamic Theory of Racial Income Differences," in *Women, Minorities, and Employment Discrimination,* ed. P. A. Wallace and A. Le Mund (Lexington, Mass.: Lexington Books, 1977); James S. Coleman, Thomas Hoffer, and Sally Kilgore, *High School Achievement: Public, Catholic, and Private Schools Compared* (New York: Basic, 1982); James S. Coleman and Thomas Hoffer, *Public and Private High Schools: The Impact of Communities* (New York: Basic, 1987); Glenn Loury, "Why Should We Care about Group Inequality?" *So-*

cial Philosophy and Policy 5 (1987): 249–71; James S. Coleman, "Social Capital in the Formation of Human Capital," American Journal of Sociology 94, Supplement (1988): S95–S120; James S. Coleman, Foundations of Social Theory (Cambridge: Harvard University Press, 1990), 300–321; Robert D. Putnam, "Bowling Alone: America's Declining Social Capital," Journal of Democracy 6, no. 1 (Jan. 1995): 65–78, and his subsequent book, Bowling Alone: The Collapse and Revival of American Community. Putnam's arguments about "bowling alone" were foreshadowed by his Making Democracy Work: Civic Traditions in Modern Italy (Princeton: Princeton University Press, 1993), which tied the concept of social capital in a much more central manner to the fate of democracy in different social formations.

9. Andrew Greeley, "Coleman Revisited: Religious Structures as Sources of Social Capital," American Behavioral Scientist 40, no. 5 (Mar./Apr. 1997): 587–94; Alejandro Portes, "Social Capital: Its Origins and Applications in Modern Sociology," Annual Reviews in Sociology 24 (1998): 1–24.

10. On the distinction between parental involvement and parental engagement, see Shirley, Community Organizing, 70–76.

11. Anthony S. Bryk, Valerie E. Lee, and Peter B. Holland, Catholic Schools and the Common Good (Cambridge: Harvard University Press, 1993), 306–08, 378.

12. On the problems created by school reform efforts for classroom teachers, see Seymour Sarason, The Predictable Failure of School Reform (San Francisco: Jossey-Bass, 1990); Andy Hargreaves, Changing Teachers, Changing Times: Teachers' Work and Culture in the Postmodern Age (New York: Teachers College Press, 1994); and Donna E. Muncey and Patrick J. McQuillan, Reform and Resistance in Schools and Classrooms: An Ethnographic Portrait of the Coalition of Essential Schools (New Haven: Yale University Press, 1996); McNeil, Contradictions of School Reform.

13. Key recent texts on civil society include Jean Louise Cohen and Andrew Arato, Civil Society and Political Theory (Cambridge: MIT University Press, 1992), and John A. Hall, ed., Civil Society: Theory, History, Comparison (Cambridge, Mass.: Polity, 1995). My own interpretation of civil society has been influenced by the work of Alexis de Tocqueville, particularly Democracy in America (Garden City, N.Y.: Anchor, 1969) and The Old Régime and the French Revolution (Garden City, N.Y.: Anchor, 1955).

14. Arnoldo DeLeón, The Tejano Community, 1836–1900 (Albuquerque: University of New Mexico Press, 1982); James Talmadge Moore, Through Fire and Flood: The Catholic Church in Frontier Texas, 1836–1900 (College Station: Texas A&M University Press, 1992), 186–99.

15. See Américo Paredes, *With His Pistol in His Hand.* (Austin: University of Texas Press, 1958), and Robert J. Rosenbaum, *Mexicano Resistance in the Southwest: "The Sacred Right of Self-Preservation"* (Austin: University of Texas Press, 1981).

16. Evan Anders, *Boss Rule in South Texas: The Progressive Era* (Austin: University of Texas Press, 1982); "Poorest Area in America Begins to Fight Its Way Up," *U.S. News and World Report*, 7 Oct. 1974, 45–48.

17. Steven A. Holmes, "Immigration Fueling Cities' Strong Growth," *New York Times*, 1 Jan. 1998.

18. On social and economic indicators in the Valley, see Robert H. Wilson and Peter Menzies, "The *Colonias* Water Bill: Communities Demanding Change," in *Public Policy and Community: Activism and Governance in Texas* (Austin: University of Texas Press, 1997), ed. Robert H. Wilson, 229; on problems impacting South Texas in the wake of NAFTA, see Sam Howe Verhovek, "Benefits of Free-Trade Pact Bypass Texas Border Towns," *New York Times*, 23 June 1998; see also Jessica Portner, "Border Ills," *Education Week*, 31 May 2000, 29.

19. On the education of Latinos nationally, see Kenneth J. Meier and Joseph Stewart, Jr., *The Politics of Hispanic Education* (Albany: State University of New York Press, 1991), and Herbert Grossman, *Educating Hispanic Students: Cultural Implications for Instruction, Classroom Management, Counseling and Assessment* (Springfield, Ill.: Charles C. Thomas, 1984); on the disproportionate economic impact of a restructuring economy on Latinos, see Jorge Chapa, "The Myth of Hispanic Progress: Trends in the Educational and Economic Attainment of Mexican Americans," *Journal of Hispanic Policy* 4 (1989–90): 3–18, and Vilma Ortiz, "The Mexican-Origin Population: Permanent Working Class or Emerging Middle Class?" in *Ethnic Los Angeles*, ed. Roger Waldinger and Mehdi Bozorgmehr (New York: Russell Sage, 1996); on health care and Latinos, see Ruth E. Zambrana, ed., *Work, Family, and Health: Latina Women in Transition* (Bronx, N.Y.: Hispanic Research Center, 1982), Antonia Darder and Rodolfo D. Torres, eds., *The Latino Studies Reader: Culture, Economy, and Society* (Malden, Mass.: Blackwell, 1998), and Lyndon B. Johnson School of Public Affairs, *The Health of Mexican-Americans in South Texas* (Austin: University of Texas, 1979). On education in a globalizing economy, see Ray Marshall and Marc Tucker, *Thinking for a Living: Work, Skills, and the Future of the American Economy* (New York: Basic, 1992), and Richard J. Murnane and Frank Levy, *Teaching the New Basic Skills: Principles for Educating Children to Thrive in a Changing Economy* (New York: Free Press, 1996).

20. There have been many important contributions to qualitative research in education in recent years. For valuable summaries, see Mar-

garet D. LeCompte, Wendy L. Millroy, and Judith Preissle, eds., *The Handbook of Qualitative Research in Education* (New York: Academic Press, 1992); see also Elliot W. Eisner, *The Enlightened Eye: Qualitative Inquiry and the Enhancement of Educational Practice* (New York: Macmillan, 1991).

21. See Paredes' seminal essay, "On Ethnographic Work among Minority Groups: A Folklorist's Perspective," in his *Folklore and Culture*; see also José E. Limón, *The Return of the Mexican Ballad: Américo Paredes and His Anthropological Text as Persuasive Political Performance*, SCCR Working Paper No. 16 (Stanford: Stanford Center for Chicano Research, Stanford University, 1986), and *Dancing with the Devil: Society and Cultural Poetics in Mexican-American South Texas* (Madison: University of Wisconsin Press, 1994).

CHAPTER I

1. See David Montejano, *Anglos and Mexicans in the Making of Texas, 1836-1986*, and Rodolfo Acuña, *Occupied America: A History of Chicanos* (New York: Harper & Row, 1988).

2. See Emilio Zamora, *The World of the Mexican Worker in Texas* (College Station: Texas A&M University Press); Guadalupe San Miguel Jr., *"Let All of Them Take Heed": Mexican Americans and the Campaign for Educational Equality in Texas, 1910-1981* (Austin: University of Texas Press, 1987); Benjamin Márquez, *LULAC: The Evolution of a Mexican American Political Organization* (Austin: University of Texas Press, 1993).

3. Montejano, *Anglos and Mexicans*, 284.

4. Ibid. On the conflicted role of the Catholic Church in regard to the strike, see also Saul E. Bronder, *Social Justice and Church Authority: The Public Life of Archbishop Robert E. Lucey* (Philadelphia: Temple University Press, 1982).

5. Carlos Muñoz Jr., *Youth, Identity, Power: The Chicano Movement* (New York: Verso, 1989); Armando Navarro, *Mexican American Youth Organization: Avant-garde of the Chicano Movement in Texas* (Austin: University of Texas Press, 1995), 109, 224. On Catholic Church activism, see Bronder, *Social Justice and Church Authority*, and Charles R. Morris, *American Catholic: The Saints and Sinners Who Built America's Most Powerful Church* (New York: Random House, 1997), 261-66.

6. Montejano, *Anglos and Mexicans*, 289-92.

7. Bishop John Joseph Fitzpatrick, interview by author, Edinburg, Tex., 30 Mar. 1998. Unless otherwise noted, all interviews were by the author.

8. There is an extensive literature on Saul Alinsky and the Indus-

trial Areas Foundation. The major writings include two books by Alinsky—*Reveille for Radicals* (Chicago: University of Chicago Press, 1946) and *Rules for Radicals* (New York: Vintage, 1971)—and a biography by Sanford D. Horwitt, *Let Them Call Me Rebel: Saul Alinsky—His Life and Legacy* (New York: Vintage, 1992). On the origins of the Texas organizations, see Dennis Shirley, *Community Organizing for Urban School Reform*, 32–96. On COPS, see Joseph D. Sekul, "Communities Organized for Public Service: Citizen Power and Public Policy in San Antonio," in *The Politics of San Antonio: Community, Progress, and Power* (Lincoln: University of Nebraska Press, 1983), ed. David R. Johnson, John A. Booth, and Richard J. Harris; Mary Beth Rogers, *Cold Anger: A Story of Faith and Power Politics* (Denton: University of North Texas, 1990); Jeffrey M. Berry, Kent E. Portney, and Ken Thomson, *The Rebirth of Urban Democracy* (Washington, D.C.: Brookings Institution, 1993); Heywood T. Sanders, "Communities Organized for Public Services and Neighborhood Revitalization in San Antonio," in *Public Policy and Community: Activism and Governance in Texas* (Austin: University of Texas Press, 1997), ed. Robert H. Wilson; Shirley, *Community Organizing*.

9. Ernie Cortés, interview, Cambridge, Mass., 3 Dec. 1997.

10. On "assisted performance," see Lev S. Vygotsky, *Mind in Society: The Development of Higher Psychological Processes* (Cambridge: Harvard University Press, 1978), and Roland G. Tharp and Ronald Gallimore, *Rousing Minds to Life: Teaching, Learning, and Schooling in Social Context* (Cambridge: Cambridge University Press, 1988).

11. Ernie Cortés, interview, Cambridge, Mass., 15 Oct. 1998.

12. Scott Lind, "Politicians Enlisted to Raise Valley Standards," *Texas Observer*, 10 Jan. 1986, 14–15.

13. Ernie Cortés, interview, Austin, Tex., 28 Feb. 1999; Javier Parra, interview, Austin, Tex., 1 Mar. 1999. Among the best historical studies of Valley politics are Evan Anders, *Boss Rule in South Texas: The Progressive Era*; Montejano, *Anglos and Mexicans*; and Zamora, *World of the Mexican Worker*.

14. Tim McCluskey, interview, Edinburg, Tex., 29 Mar. 1998.

15. Ann Richards, telephone conversation with author, 5 Nov. 1998; Ed Asher, "Two Years Later, Interfaith Commands Respect," *Brownsville Herald*, 30 Mar. 1986; Ed Asher, "White, Water Board Members Tour Valley Colonias," *Brownsville Herald*, 3 June 1986.

16. For background on the school-finance litigation and reform in Texas, see Jonathan Kozol, *Savage Inequalities: Children in America's Schools* (New York: Crown, 1991), 206–33; Thomas Toch, *In the Name of Excellence* (New York: Oxford University Press, 1991), 72–95; Gregory G. Rocha and Robert H. Webking, *Politics and Public Education:* Edgewood

v. Kirby and the Reform of Public School Financing in Texas (Minneapolis: West, 1992); Linda McNeil, *Contradictions of School Reform: Educational Costs of Standardized Testing*, 153–88.

17. On the IAF's work with school reform in Chicago, see John Hall Fish, *Black Power/White Control* (Princeton: Princeton University Press, 1973), and Arthur M. Brazier, *Black Self-Determination: The Story of the Woodlawn Organization* (Grand Rapids, Mich.: William B. Eerdmans, 1969).

18. On the Texas IAF and school reform, see Richard Lavine, "School Finance Reform in Texas, 1983–1995," in *Public Policy and Community*, ed. Wilson, 119–65; on the impact of House Bill 72 on academic achievement, see Ronald F. Ferguson, "Paying for Public Education: New Evidence on How and Why Money Matters," *Harvard Journal of Legislation* 28, no. 2 (1991): 465–91.

19. Ernesto Cortés, "Reweaving the Fabric: The Iron Rule and the IAF Strategy for Power and Politics," in *Interwoven Destinies: Cities and the Nation*, ed. Henry G. Cisneros (New York: W. W. Norton, 1993), 300–301; Cortes, interview, 15 Oct. 1998.

20. Cortés, "Reweaving the Fabric," 302–03.

21. Carmen Anaya, interview, Pharr, Tex., 27 Apr. 1997. Carmen Anaya's life shares many similarities with the lives of Mexicana and Chicana women documented in the anthology *Women on the U.S.-Mexico Border: Responses to Change*, ed. Vicki L. Ruiz and Susan Tiano (Boston: Allen and Unwin, 1987).

22. Carmen Anaya, interview, Pharr, Tex., 24 Apr. 1997; Richards, telephone conversation.

23. On the Uribe incident, see Consuelo Tovar, "Senator Learns We Mean Business," in *Organizing for Change: IAF, 50 Years*, ed. Cynthia Perry (Franklin Square, N.Y.: Industrial Areas Foundation, 1990).

24. Parra, interview.

25. Lind, "Politicians Enlisted," 14; Virginia Armstrong, "Brand: Interfaith Losing Support," *Monitor*, 25 May 1984; Othal Brand, telephone conversation, 16 Oct. 1998.

26. "Interfaith Supports Colonia Bill, Opposes CP&L Rate Hike," *Monitor*, 12 Feb. 1989.

27. Diane Smith, "Valley Interfaith Wins Friends, Foes, in 10 Activist Years," *Monitor*, 13 Feb. 1994.

28. Virginia Armstrong, "Interfaith Supports 66 Million Project," *Monitor*, 8 Feb. 1984; "Interfaith Leaders, Brand Clash at Meeting," *Monitor*, 4 Mar. 1984; and "Montalvo Supports Interfaith Plan," *Monitor*, 30 Mar. 1984.

29. Heather Ball and J. Michael Patrick, "The Jobs of South Texas: Still Frozen" (Austin: Texas Department of Agriculture, 1985).

30. Cortés, interview, 28 Feb. 1999.

31. Ed Asher, "Pauken Urges Catholics to Stop Donating to Inter-faith," *Monitor*, 14 Apr. 1986.

32. Ed Asher, "Church Cuts Ties to Interfaith," *Monitor*, 26 Apr. 1984; Ed Asher, "Group Wants Church Out of Interfaith," *Monitor*, 17 Aug. 1984; Virginia Armstrong, "Members Oppose McAllen Church's Ties to Interfaith," *Monitor*, Oct. 21, 1984.

33. Tom Pauken, telephone conversation, 15 Jan. 1999; Tom Pauken, *The Thirty Years War: The Politics of the Sixties Generation* (Ottawa, Ill.: Jameson Books, 1995), 178–82. On the early history of COPS, see Shirley, *Community Organizing*, 39–53.

34. Concerned Citizens Committee of the Rio Grande Valley, "A Second Look at Valley Interfaith" (1984, photocopy), 3–4; Smith, "Valley Interfaith Wins Friends, Foes"; Lind, "Politicians Enlisted," 15.

35. Bill Hobby, interview, Houston, Tex., 28 May 1996; Connie Maheshwari, interview, Edinburg, Tex., 29 Mar. 1998.

36. Peter Applebome, "Changing Texas Politics at Its Roots, *New York Times*, 31 May 1988; Ralph K. M. Haurwitz, "Colonias Legislation Goes to Governor," *Austin American-Statesman*, 25 May 1999; Richards, telephone conversation; Allen Essex and Travis M. Whitehead, "Hutchison Visits Colonias," *Valley Morning Star*, 20 July 1999; Kay Bailey Hutchison, "Cleaning Up the Colonias," *Austin American-Statesman*, 27 July 1999.

37. Anaya, interview, 24 Apr. 1997. On the study groups on indigent care, see Rogers, *Cold Anger*, 45, and Pat Wong, "The Indigent Health Care Package," in *Public Policy and Community*, ed. Wilson, 95–118.

CHAPTER 2

1. Salvador Flores, interview, Pharr, Tex., 22 May 1997. On flooding in the colonias, see Robert H. Wilson and Peter Menzies, "The *Colonias* Water Bill: Communities Demanding Change," in *Public Policy and Community: Activism and Governance in Texas*, ed. Robert H. Wilson, 232.

2. Salvador Flores and Esmerejildo Ramos, interview, Pharr, Tex., 25 Aug. 1999; Cam Rossie, "Religious Alliance Forms in Valley," *Valley Morning Star*, 14 Aug. 1983.

3. Salvador Flores, interview, Pharr, Tex., 3 June 1997.

4. Salvador Flores, interview, Pharr, Tex., 16 Dec. 1997. See Ronald F. Ferguson, "Paying for Public Education: New Evidence on How and Why Money Matters," *Harvard Journal of Legislation* 28 (1991): 465–91. For an example of the manner in which business leaders receive pub-

lic recognition but community groups do not, see John Gittelsohn, "Lessons from the Lone Star State: Business Played Role in Texas Reform," *Orange County Register,* 18 May 1997.

5. Salvador Flores, interview, Pharr, Tex., 29 Mar. 1998.

6. Salvador Flores, interview, Pharr, Tex., 22 Sept. 1997.

7. Salvador Flores, interview, Pharr, Tex., 19 Nov. 1997.

8. On the struggle to equalize school funding, see Richard Lavine, "School Finance Reform in Texas, 1983–1995," in *Public Policy and Community,* ed. Wilson; Gregory G. Rocha and Robert H. Webking, *Politics and Public Education:* Edgewood v. Kirby *and the Reform of Public School Financing in Texas.*

9. Salvador Flores, interview, McAllen, Tex., 23 Aug. 1999.

10. Flores, interview, 22 Sept. 1997.

11. Ibid.

12. Flores, interview, 16 Dec. 1997.

13. Flores, interview, 23 Aug. 1997.

14. Yolanda Castillo, "Palmer Elementary School Parental Involvement Plan" (Palmer Elementary School, Pharr, Tex., photocopy).

15. Yolanda Castillo, interview, Pharr, Tex., 14 Dec. 1997.

16. Flores, interview, 22 Sept. 1997.

17. Rosario Bustos, interview, Pharr, Tex., 24 Apr. 1997.

18. Rick Dailey, "Millions in Funds Offer a Little Hope," *Valley Morning Star,* 22 Mar. 1997.

19. Gregg Wendorf, "Tired Yet of Local Politics?" *Advance News Journal,* 14 May 1997.

20. Salvador Flores, interview, Pharr, Tex., 30 Apr. 1997.

21. The distinction between parental involvement and parental engagement was first made clear to me by Elsy Fierro-Suttmiller, an IAF organizer with the El Paso Interreligious Sponsoring Organization in 1994.

22. Yolanda Castillo, interview, Pharr, Tex., 16 Nov. 1997; Salvador Flores, interview, Pharr, Tex., 26 Aug. 1999.

CHAPTER 3

1. Lesley Whitlock, interview, Alamo, Tex., 17 Nov. 1997.

2. René Ramirez, interview, Pharr, Tex., 25 Apr. 1997.

3. Ibid.

4. Ibid.

5. Linda Swan, "Teachers Getting Parents Involved," *Monitor,* 3 Sept. 1993.

6. David Cortez, interview, Alamo, Tex., 2 June 1997.

7. Ibid.

8. Allen Cox, interview, Alamo, Tex., 15 Dec. 1997; René Ramirez, interview, Pharr, Tex., 22 May 1997.

9. Oliver Nayola, interview, Alamo, Tex., 23 May 1997.

10. Ramirez, interview, 22 May 1997.

11. Elizabeth Valdez, interview, Edinburg, Tex., 28 Mar. 1998.

12. Ramirez, interview, 22 May 1997; Valdez, interview; Barbara King, "Sixth Graders Will Stay at Alamo Middle School," *Monitor*, 1 Apr. 1994.

13. Nayola, interview, 23 May 1997.

14. Cortez, interview, 2 June 1997.

15. Ibid.

16. Diana Hinojosa, interview, Alamo, Tex., 25 Aug. 1999.

17. Julia D. Nava, "School Has New Discipline Program," *Monitor*, 23 Aug. 1999; Dina Herrera, "Alamo Middle School Launches Discipline Program," *Advance News Journal*, 18 Aug. 1999.

18. Rosi Ruiz, interview, Alamo, Tex., 26 Aug. 1999.

CHAPTER 4

1. Connie Maheshwari, interview, McAllen, Tex., 18 Nov. 1997.

2. This generalization about churches in Pharr and Alamo is not entirely accurate, for clergy there have come forth intermittently to support their neighborhood schools and their communities. Father Pat McDonald at Resurrection Catholic Church in Alamo, for example, worked with Alamo Middle School on Alliance School grants as a community liaison, and he also spoke before the Texas Water Commission in Austin in Apr. 1997 to impress upon the commission the urgency of sewer lines for colonias such as Mexico Chiquito and South Tower Estates in south Alamo. Nonetheless, as the narrative will make evident, the role of Father Bart Flaat and Sister Maria Sanchez at Saint Joseph's the Worker does appear to belong in another league altogether.

3. Father Bart Flaat, interview, McAllen, Tex., 21 May 1997.

4. Ibid.

5. Ibid. *Comunidades de base,* or "Christian base communities," emerged out of a movement for theological renewal in Latin American Catholicism in the 1970s and 1980s known as "liberation theology." See Gustavo Gutiérrez, *A Theology of Liberation* (Maryknoll, N.Y.: Orbis, 1988); James B. Nickloff, ed., *Gustavo Gutiérrez: Essential Writings* (Minneapolis: Fortress Press, 1996); Sergio Torres and John Eagleson, eds., *The Challenge of Basic Christian Communities* (Maryknoll, N.Y.: Orbis, 1981); Alfred T. Hennelly, "Grassroots Communities: A New Model of Church?" in *Tracing the Spirit: Communities, Social Action, and Theological Reflection,* ed. James E. Hug (New York: Paulist Press,

1983); Pablo Galdámez, *Faith of a People: The Life of a Basic Christian Community in El Salvador* (Maryknoll, N.Y.: Orbis, 1986).

6. Sister Maria Sanchez, interview, McAllen, Tex., 27 Mar. 1998.

7. Connie Maheshwari, interview, McAllen, Tex., 16 Dec. 1997.

8. Ibid.

9. Ibid.

10. Ibid. On Zavala Elementary School, see Dennis Shirley, *Community Organizing for Urban School Reform*, 147–66; and Richard J. Murnane and Frank Levy, *Teaching the New Basic Skills: Principles for Educating Children to Thrive in a Changing Economy*, 80–108.

11. Estela Sosa-Garza, interview, McAllen, Tex., 23 May 1997.

12. Sister Pearl Ceasar, interview, Mercedes, Tex., 24 Apr. 1997.

13. Diana Garza, interview, McAllen, Tex., 18 Nov. 1997.

14. Raquel Guzman, interview, McAllen, Tex., 18 Nov. 1997.

15. Ibid.

16. Ibid.

17. Ibid. The concept of schools as microsocieties dates back at least to John Dewey's laboratory school at the University of Chicago. For the specific model implemented at Sam Houston, see George H. Richmond, *The Micro-Society School: A Real World in Miniature* (New York: Harper & Row, 1973), and George H. Richmond and Carolynn King Richmond, *The Microsociety Handbook* (Philadelphia: n.p., n.d.).

18. Sarai Oviedo, Mary Ann Rosales, and Leticia Casas, interview, McAllen, Tex., 16 Dec. 1997.

19. Mary Vela, interview, McAllen, Tex., 5 May 1998.

20. Mary Ann Rosales, interview, McAllen, Tex., 24 Aug. 1999.

21. Maheshwari, interview, 16 Dec. 1997.

22. Connie Maheshwari, telephone conversation, 7 June 1999.

CHAPTER 5

1. Rickey Dailey, "Moses Vows to Back Funding for Alliance Schools," *Monitor*, 18 Feb. 1997.

2. See Paul Clopton, Wayne Bishop, and David Klein, "Statewide Mathematics Assessment in Texas" <*http://mathematicallycorrect. com/lonestar.html*>; Sandra Stotsky, "Analysis of the Texas Reading Tests" <*http://www.taxresearch.org/read.html*>; Peter Schrag, "Too Good to Be True," *American Prospect*, 3 Jan. 2000, 46–49. Only one of the surveys is published; it is by Stephen P. Gordon and Marianne Reese, entitled "High Stakes Testing: Worth the Price?" *Journal of School Leadership* 7 (July 1997): 345–68. The second is by James V. Hoffman, Lori Assaf, Julie Pennington, and Scott G. Paris, and is entitled "High Stakes Testing in Reading: Today in Texas, Tomorrow?" The first three au-

thors are at the University of Texas at Austin and the fourth is at the University of Michigan. The third survey was conducted by Walt Haney of Boston College and is described in "The Myth of the Texas Miracle in Education," *Education Policy Analysis Archives* 8, no. 41 <http://olam.ed.asa.edu/epaa/v8n41/>. The core of Haney's deposition for MALDEF is described in his "Preliminary Report on Texas Assessment of Academic Skills Exit Test (TAAS-X)" (Dec. 1998, photocopy).

3. See the Dana Center website at <http://www.utdanacenter. org>; David Grissimer and Ann Flanagan, "Exploring Rapid Achievement Gains in North Carolina and Texas" (Washington, D.C.: National Education Goals Panel, 1998); and Tyce Palmaffy, "The Gold Star State: How Texas Jumped to the Head of the Class in Elementary School Achievement," *Policy Review*, no. 88 (Mar.–Apr. 1998) <http://www. policyreview.com//mar98/goldstar.html>.

4. Connie Maheshwari, interview, McAllen, Tex., 28 Mar. 1998; Connie Maheshwari, interview, McAllen, Tex., 18 Nov. 1997.

5. Sister Pearl Ceasar, interview, Mercedes, Tex., 23 May 1997; Jim Drake (Jan. 1986, photocopy); Father Bart Flaat, interview, McAllen, Tex., 24 Apr. 1997.

6. See Maxine Baca Zinn, "Mexican American Women in the Social Sciences," *Signs: Journal of Women in Culture and Society* 8, no. 2 (winter 1982): 259–72; Alfredo Mirandé and Evangelina Enríquez, *La Chicana: The Mexican American Woman* (Chicago: University of Chicago Press, 1986); Carlos Vélez-Ibáñez, *Border Visions: Mexican Cultures of the Southwest United States*; Pierrette Hondagneu-Sotelo, *Gendered Transitions: Mexican Experiences of Immigration*. For Handagneu-Sotelo's thesis on the role of immigration, see also Susan González Baker et al., "U.S. Immigration Policies and Trends: The Growing Importance of Migration from Mexico," in *Crossings*, 81–105, esp. 95–101.

7. For Latina feminist theology, see Ada María Isasi-Díaz and Yolanda Tarango, *Hispanic Women: Prophetic Voice in the Church* (San Francisco: Harper & Row, 1988); Ada María Isasi-Díaz, *Mujerista Theology: A Theology for the Twenty-First Century* (Maryknoll, N.Y.: Orbis, 1996); Elsa Tamez, ed., *Through Her Eyes: Women's Theology from Latin America* (Maryknoll, N.Y.: Orbis, 1989); Gloria Inés Loya, "The Hispanic Woman: Pasionaria and Pastora of the Hispanic Community," in *Frontiers of Hispanic Theology in the United States*, ed. Allan Figueroa Deck (Maryknoll, N.Y.: Orbis, 1992), 124–33; María Pilar Aquino, *Our Cry for Life: Feminist Theology from Latin America* (Maryknoll, N.Y.: Orbis, 1993).

8. Henry Giroux, *Teachers as Intellectuals: Toward a Critical Pedagogy of Learning* (New York: Bergin and Garvey, 1988); Susan L.

Lytle and Marilyn Cochran-Smith, "Teacher Research as a Way of Knowing," *Harvard Educational Review* 62, no. 4 (winter 1992): 447–74; Linda McNeil, *Contradictions of Control: School Structure and School Knowledge* (New York: Routledge and Kegan Paul, 1986).

9. Leticia Casa, Mary Vela, and Susanna Sarmiento, email to author, 27 Feb. 1998.

10. Julie A. White and Gary Wehlage, "Community Collaboration: If It Is Such a Good Idea, Why Is It So Hard to Do?" *Educational Evaluation and Policy Analysis* 17, no. 1, (spring 1995): 23–38, quote from 34.

11. On changing definitions of freedom in American history, see Eric Foner, *The Story of American Freedom* (New York: W. W. Norton, 1998).

12. Luis C. Moll and James B. Greenberg, "Creating Zones of Possibilities: Combining Social Contexts for Instruction," in *Vygotsky and Education: Instructional Implications and Applications of Sociohistorical Pyschology*, ed. Luis C. Moll (Cambridge: Cambridge University Press, 1990), 319–48.

13. Joyce L. Epstein, "School and Family Partnerships," in *Encyclopedia of Educational Research*, ed. M. C. Alkin, 6th ed. (New York: Macmillan, 1992), 1139–51; Concha Delgado-Gaitan, *Literacy for Empowerment: The Role of Parents in Children's Education;* James Comer, *School Power: Implications of an Intervention Project* (New York: Free Press, 1980); Sarah Lawrence Lightfoot, *Worlds Apart: Relationships between Families and Schools* (New York: Basic, 1978); Lawrence Steinberg, *Beyond the Classroom* (New York: Simon and Schuster, 1996); Seymour Sarason, *Parental Involvement and the Political Principle: Why the Existing Governance Structure of Schools Should Be Abolished* (San Francisco: Jossey-Bass, 1995).

14. Deborah Meier, *The Power of Their Ideas: Lessons for America from a Small School in Harlem* (Boston: Beacon Press, 1995), 32–33.

15. On social constructivism see Lev S. Vygotsky, *Mind in Society: The Development of Higher Psychological Processes;* Moll, *Vygotsky and Education.*

16. Frank Levy and Richard Murnane, *Teaching the New Basic Skills: Principles for Educating Children to Thrive in a Changing Economy.*

17. Jonathan Kozol, *Savage Inequalities: Children in America's Schools*, 4.

18. Dennis Shirley, *Community Organizing for Urban School Reform*, 97–116, 208–09, 217–19.

19. On the benefits of religiosity for children, see Norman Garmezy, "Stressors of Childhood," in *Stress, Coping, and Development in Children*, ed. Norman Garmezy and Michael Rutter (New York:

McGraw-Hill, 1983), 43–84; William Damon, *Greater Expectations: Overcoming the Culture of Indulgence in America's Homes and Schools* (New York: Free Press, 1995), 81–93; Peter L. Benson, *All Kids Are Our Kids: What Communities Must Do to Raise Caring and Responsible Children and Adolescents* (San Francisco: Jossey-Bass, 1997), 201–04.

20. Barry A. Kosmin and Seymour P. Lachman, *One Nation under God: Religion in Contemporary American Society* (New York: Harmony, 1993), 9, 138–39; Roberto O. González and Michael J. LaVelle, *The Hispanic Catholic in the United States: A Sociocultural and Religious Profile* (New York: Enquire Press, 1985), 126–31.

21. Connie Maheshwari, interview, McAllen, Tex., 16 Dec. 1997.

BIBLIOGRAPHY

Acuña, Rodolfo. *Occupied America: A History of Chicanos.* New York: Harper & Row, 1988.

Airasian, Peter W., and George F. Madaus. "Linking Testing and Instruction: Policy Issues." *Journal of Eduational Measurement* 20, no. 2 (summer 1983).

Alinsky, Saul. *Reveille for Radicals.* Chicago: University of Chicago Press, 1946.

————. *Rules for Radicals.* New York: Vintage, 1971.

Anders, Evan. *Boss Rule in South Texas: The Progressive Era.* Austin: University of Texas Press, 1982.

Aquino, María Pilar. *Our Cry for Life: Feminist Theology from Latin America.* Maryknoll, N.Y.: Orbis, 1993.

Arato, Andrew, and Jean Louise Cohen. *Civil Society and Political Theory.* Cambridge: MIT University Press, 1992.

Baker, Susan González, Frank D. Bean, Augustin Escobar Latapi, and Sidney Weintraub. "U.S. Immigration Policies and Trends: The Growing Importance of Migration from Mexico." In *Crossings: Mexican Immigration in Interdisciplinary Perspectives,* edited by Marcelo M. Suárez-Orozco, 81–105. Cambridge: Harvard University Press, 1998.

Ball, Heather, and J. Michael Patrick. *The Jobs of South Texas: Still Frozen.* Austin: Texas Department of Agriculture, 1985.

Bean, Frank D., Roberto O. de la Garza, Bryan R. Roberts, and Sidney Weintraub, eds. *At the Crossroads: Mexico and the U.S. Immigration Policy.* Lanham, Md.: Rowman and Littlefield, 1997.

Becker, Gary S. *Human Capital: A Theoretical and Empirical Analysis with Special Reference to Education.* New York: National Bureau of Economic Research, 1964.

Benson, Peter. *All Kids Are Our Kids: What Communities Must Do to*

Raise Caring and Responsible Children and Adolescents. San Francisco: Jossey-Bass, 1997.

Berry, Jeffrey M., Kent E. Portney, and Ken Thomson. *The Rebirth of Urban Democracy.* Washington, D.C.: Brookings Institution, 1993.

Bradsher, Keith. "Gap in Wealth in U.S. Called Widest in West." *New York Times,* 17 April 1995. A1.

———. "Low Ranking for Poor American Children: U.S. Youth among Worst Off in Study of 18 Industrialized Nations." *New York Times,* 14 August 1995. A7.

Brazier, Arthur M. *Black Self-determination: The Story of the Woodlawn Organization.* Grand Rapids, Mich.: William B. Eerdmans, 1969.

Brondo, Saul E. *Social Justice and Church Authority: The Public Life of Archbishop Robert E. Lucy.* Philadelphia: Temple University Press, 1982.

Bryk, Anthony S., Valerie E. Lee, and Peter B. Holland. *Catholic Schools and the Common Good.* Cambridge: Harvard University Press, 1993.

Chapa, Jorge. "The Myth of Hispanic Progress: Trends in the Educational and Economic Attainment of Mexican Americans." *Journal of Hispanic Policy* 4 (1989–90): 3–18.

Chase-Lansdale, P. Lindsay, and Jeanne Brooks-Gunn. *Escape from Poverty: What Makes a Difference for Children?* New York: Cambridge University Press, 1995.

Cibulka, James G. "Conclusion: Toward an Interpretation of School, Family, and Community Connections: Policy Changes." In *Coordination among Schools, Families, and Communities: Prospects for Educational Reform,* edited by James G. Cibulka and William J. Kritek, 403–35. Albany: State University of New York Press, 1996.

Cohen, Jean L., and Andrew Arato. *Civil Society and Political Theory.* Cambridge: MIT University Press, 1992.

Coleman, James S. *Foundations of Social Theory.* Cambridge: Harvard University Press, 1990.

———. "Social Capital in the Formation of Human Capital." *American Journal of Sociology* 94, Supplement (1988): S95–S120.

Coleman, James S., and Thomas Hoffer. *Public and Private High Schools: The Impact of Communities.* New York: Basic, 1987.

Coleman, James S., Thomas Hoffer, and Sally Kilgore. *High School Achievement: Public, Catholic, and Private Schools Compared.* New York: Basic, 1982.

Comer, James. *School Power: Implications of an Intervention Project.* New York: Free Press, 1980.

Cortés Jr., Ernesto, "Reweaving the Fabric: The Iron Rule and the IAF Strategy for Power and Politics." In *Interwoven Destinies: Cities and the Nation,* edited by Henry G. Cisneros, 294–319. New York: W. W. Norton, 1993.

Damon, William. *Greater Expectations: Overcoming the Culture of Indulgence in America's Homes and Schools.* New York: Free Press, 1995.

Darder, Antonia, and Rodolfo D. Torres, eds. *The Latino Studies Reader: Culture, Economy, and Society.* Malden, Mass.: Blackwell, 1998.

De Anda, Roberto M., ed. *Chicanas and Chicanos in Contemporary Society.* Boston: Allyn and Bacon, 1996.

De León, Arnold. *The Tejano Community, 1869–1900.* Albuquerque: University of New Mexico Press, 1982.

Delgado-Gaitan, Concha. *Literacy for Empowerment: The Role of Parents in Children's Education.* Philadelphia: Falmer, 1990.

Dentler, Robert A. *Hosting Newcomers: Structuring Educational Opportunities for Immigrant Children.* New York: Teachers College Press, 1997.

Driscol, Mary E. "Thinking like a Fish: The Implications of the Image of the School Community for Connections between Parents and Schools." In *Transforming Schools,* edited by Peter W. Cookson Jr. and Barbara Snyder, 209–36. New York: Garland Publishing, 1995.

Eagleson, John, and Sergio Torres, eds. *The Challenge of Basic Christian Communities.* Maryknoll, N.Y.: Orbis, 1981.

Eisner, Elliot W. *The Enlightened Eye: Qualitative Inquiry and the Enhancement of Educational Practice.* New York: Macmillan, 1991.

Elshtain, Jean Bethke. *Democracy on Trial.* New York: Basic, 1995.

Epstein, Joyce L. "School and Family Partnerships." In *Encyclopedia of Educational Research,* edited by M. C. Alkin, 1139–51. 6th ed. New York: Macmillan, 1992.

Ferguson, Ronald F. "Paying for Public Education: New Evidence on How and Why Money Matters." *Harvard Journal of Legislation* 28, no. 2 (1991): 465–91.

Fish, John H. *Black Power/White Control.* Princeton: Princeton University Press.

Foner, Eric. *The Story of American Freedom.* New York: W. W. Norton, 1998.

Galdamez, Pablo. *Faith of a People: The Life of a Basic Christian Community in El Salvador.* Maryknoll, N.Y.: Orbis, 1986.

Gallimore, Ronald, and Roland G. Tharp. *Rousing Minds to Life: Teaching, Learning, and Schooling in Social Context.* Cambridge: Cambridge University Press, 1988.

Garcia, Mario T. *Mexican Americans: Leadership, Ideology, and Identity, 1930–1960.* New Haven: Yale University Press, 1989.

Garmezy, Norman. "Stressors of Childhood." In *Stress, Coping, and De-*

velopment in Children, edited by Norman Garmezy and Michael Rudder. New York: McGraw-Hill, 1983.

Giroux, Henry. *Teachers as Intellectuals: Toward a Critical Pedagogy of Learning.* New York: Bergin and Garvey, 1998.

Gonzalez, Roberto O., and Michael J. Lavelle. *The Hispanic Catholic in the United States: A Socio-cultural and Religious Profile.* New York: Enquire Press, 1995.

Gordon, Stephen P., and Marianne Reese. "High Stakes Testing: Worth the Price?" *Journal of School Leadership* 7 (July 1997): 345–68.

Greeley, Andrew. "Coleman Revisited: Religious Structures as Sources of Social Capital." *American Behavioral Scientist* 40, no. 5 (March–April 1997): 587–94.

Grossman, Herbert. *Educating Hispanic Students: Cultural Implications for Instruction, Classroom Management, Counseling, and Assessment.* Springfield, Ill.: Thomas C. Charles, 1984.

Gutiérrez, David, ed. *Between Two Worlds: Mexican Immigrants in the United States.* Wilmington, Del.: Scholarly Resources, 1996.

Gutiérrez, Gustavo. *A Theology of Liberation.* Maryknoll, N.Y.: Orbis, 1998.

Hall, John A., ed. *Civil Society: Theory, History, Comparison.* Cambridge, Mass.: Polity, 1995.

Haney, Walter M. "The Myth of the Texas Miracle in Education." Palmer Elementary School, Pharr, Texas. 2000. Photocopy.

Haney, Walter M. "Testing and Minorities." In *Beyond Silenced Voices: Class, Race, and Gender in United States Schools,* edited by Lois Weis and Michelle Fine, 45–73. Albany: State University of New York Press, 1993.

Haney, Walter M., Robert Lyons, and George F. Madaus. *The Fractured Marketplace for Standardized Testing.* Boston: Kluwer Academic Publishers, 1993.

Hargreaves, Andy. *Changing Teachers, Changing Times: Teachers' Work and Culture in the Postmodern Age.* New York: Teachers College Press, 1994.

Hennelly, Alfred T. "Grassroots Communities: A New Model of Church?" In *Tracing the Spirit: Communities, Social Action, and Theological Reflection,* edited by James E. Hug, 60–82. New York: Paulist Press, 1983.

Herzog, Lawrence A. *Where North Meets South: Cities, Space, and Politics on the U.S.-Mexico Border.* Austin: University of Texas Press, 1990.

Hoffman, James V., Lori Assaf, Julie Pennington, and Scott G. Paris. "High Stakes Testing in Reading: Today in Texas, Tomorrow?" 2000. Photocopy.

Holmes, Steven A. "Immigration Fueling Cities' Strong Growth." *New York Times,* 1 January 1998.

Hondagneu-Sotelo, Pierrette. *Gendered Transitions: Mexican Experiences of Immigration.* Berkeley: University of California Press, 1994.

Horwitt, Sanford D. *Let Them Call Me Rebel: Saul Alinsky—His Life and Legacy.* New York: Vintage, 1992.

Isasi-Díaz, Ada María. *Mujerista Theology: A Theology for the Twenty-First Century.* Maryknoll, N.Y.: Orbis, 1996.

Isasi-Díaz, Ada María, and Yolanda Tarango. *Hispanic Women: Prophetic Voice in the Church.* San Francisco: Harper & Row, 1988.

Johnson, David C. "Gap between Rich and Poor Found Substantially Wider." *New York Times,* 5 September 1999. A14.

Johnson, David R., John A. Booth, and Richard J. Harris, eds. *The Politics of San Antonio: Community, Progress, and Power.* Lincoln: University of Nebraska Press, 1983.

Johnson, Jean, and Steve Farkas. *Assignment Incomplete: The Unfinished Business of Education Reform.* New York: Public Agenda, 1995.

Khan, Chandra C., and Abdullah A. Khan. *Nutrition Status of Mexican American Children in the United States.* New York: Garland, 1993.

Koretz, Daniel. "Arriving in Lake Wobegon: Are Standardized Tests Exaggerating Achievement and Distorting Instruction?" *American Educator* 12, no. 2 (summer 1988): 8–15, 46–52.

Kosmin, Barry, and Seymour P. Lachman. *One Nation under God: Religion in Contemporary American Society.* New York: Harmony, 1993.

Kozol, Jonathan. *Savage Inequalities: Children in America's Schools.* New York: Crown, 1991.

Lareau, Annette. *Home Advantage: Social Class and Parental Intervention in Elementary Education.* Philadelphia: Falmer, 1989.

Lavine, Richard. "School Finance Reform in Texas, 1983–1995." In *Public Policy and Community: Activism and Governance in Texas,* edited by Robert H. Wilson, 119–65.

LeCompte, Margaret D., Wendy L. Millroy, and Judith Presille, eds. *Handbook of Qualitative Research in Education.* New York: Academic Press, 1992.

Levy, Frank. *The New Dollars and Dreams: American Incomes and Economic Change.* New York: Russell Sage, 1998.

Lightfoot, Sarah L. *Worlds Apart: Relationships between Family and Schools.* New York: Basic, 1978.

Limón, José E. *Dancing with the Devil: Society and Cultural Poetics in Mexican-American South Texas.* Madison: University of Wisconsin Press, 1994.

———. *The Return of the Mexican Ballad: Américo Paredes and His Anthropological Text as Persuasive Political Performance.* SCCR

Working Paper No. 16. Stanford: Stanford Center for Chicano Research, Stanford University, 1986.

Lind, Scott. "Politicians Enlisted to Raise Valley Standards." *Texas Observer*, no.10, January 1986.

Loury, Glenn. "A Dynamic Theory of Racial Income Differences." In *Women, Minorities, and Employment Discrimination*, edited by P. A. Wallace and A. Le Mund, 153–86. Lexington, Mass.: Lexington Books, 1977.

———. "Why Should We Care about Group Inequality?" *Social Philosophy and Policy* 5 (1987): 249–71.

Loya, Gloria Inés. "The Hispanic Woman: Pasionaria and Pastora of the Hispanic Community." In *Frontiers of Hispanic Theology in the United States*, edited by Allan Figueroa Deck, 124–33. Maryknoll, N.Y.: Orbis, 1992.

Lyte, Susan L., and Marilyn Cochran-Smith. "Teacher Research as a Way of Knowing." *Harvard Educational Review* 62, no. 4 (winter 1992): 447–74.

McNeil, Linda. *Contradictions of Control: School Structure and School Knowledge*. New York: Routledge and Kegan Paul, 1986.

———. *Contradictions of School Reform: Educational Costs of Standardized Testing*. New York: Routledge, 2000.

Madaus, George F. "The Influence of Testing on the Curriculum." In *Critical Issues in Curriculum*, edited by Laurel N. Tanner, 83–121. Chicago: University of Chicago Press, 1988.

———. "A Technological and Historical Consideration of Equity Issues Associated with Proposals to Change the Nation's Testing Policy." *Harvard Educational Review* 64, no. 1 (spring 1994): 76–95.

Mareoff, Gene I. "Altered Destinies: Making Life Better for School Children in Need." *Phi Delta Kappan* 79, no. 6 (February 1998): 425–32.

Marquez, Benjamin. *LULAC: The Evolution of a Mexican American Political Organization*. Austin: University of Texas Press, 1993.

Marshall, Ray, and Marc Tucker. *Thinking for a Living: Work, Skills, and the Future of the American Economy*. New York: Basic, 1992.

Meier, Deborah. *The Power of Their Ideas: Lessons for America from a Small School in Harlem*. Boston: Beacon Press, 1995.

Meier, Kenneth J., and Joseph Stewart Jr. *The Politics of Hispanic Education*. Albany: State University of New York Press, 1991.

Miller, L. Scott. *An American Imperative: Accelerating Minority Educational Advancement*. New Haven: Yale University Press, 1995.

Mirandé, Alfredo, and Evangelina Enríquez. *La Chicana: The Mexican-American Woman*. Chicago: University of Chicago Press, 1986.

Moll, Louis C., and James B. Greenberg. "Creating Zones of Possibilities: Combining Social Contexts for Instruction." In *Vygotsky and Educa-*

tion: *Instructional Implications and Applications of Socio-historical Psychology,* edited by Louis C. Moll, 319–48. Cambridge: Cambridge University Press, 1990.

Montejano, David. *Anglos and Mexicans in the Making of Texas, 1836–1986.* Austin: University of Texas Press, 1987.

Moore, James T. *Through Fire and Flood: The Catholic Church in Frontier Texas, 1836–1900.* College Station: Texas A&M University Press, 1992.

Moreno, José F., ed. *The Elusive Quest for Equality: One Hundred and Fifty Years of Chicano/Chicana Education.* Cambridge: Harvard Educational Review, 1999.

Morris, Charles R. *American Catholic: The Saints and the Sinners Who Built America's Most Powerful Church.* New York: Random House, 1997.

Muncey, Donna E., and Patrick J. McQuillan. *Reform and Resistance in Schools and Classrooms: An Ethnographic Portrait of the Coalition of Essential Schools.* New Haven: Yale University Press, 1996.

Muñoz Jr., Carlos. *Youth, Identity, Power: The Chicano Movement.* New York: Verso, 1989.

Murnane, Richard J., and Frank Levy. *Teaching the New Basic Skills: Principles for Educating Children to Thrive in a Changing Economy.* New York: Free Press, 1996.

National Commission on Testing and Public Policy. *From Gatekeeper to Gateway: Transforming Testing in America.* Chestnut Hill, Mass.: National Commission on Testing and Public Policy, 1990.

Navarro, Armando. *Mexican American Youth Organization: Avant-garde of the Chicano Movement in Texas.* Austin: University of Texas Press, 1995.

Nickloff, James B., ed. *Gustavo Gutiérrez: Essential Writings.* Minneapolis: Fortress Press, 1996.

Olsen, Laurie. *Made in America: Immigrant Students in Our Public Schools.* New York: New Press, 1997.

Ortiz, Vilma. "The Mexican-Origin Population: Permanent Working Class or Emerging Middle Class?" In *Ethnic Los Angeles,* edited by Roger Waldinger and Mehdi Bozorgmehr, 247–78. New York: Russell Sage, 1996.

Palmaffy, Tyce. "The Gold Star State: How Texas Jumped to the Head of the Class in Elementary School Achievement." *Policy Review* 88 (March–April 1998) <http://www.policyreview.com//mar98/goldstar.html>.

Paredes, Américo. *With His Pistol in His Hand.* Austin: University of Texas Press, 1958.

———. *Folklore and Culture on the Texas-Mexican Border*. Austin: Center for Mexican-American Studies, University of Texas, 1993.

Pauken, Tom. *The Thirty Years War: Politics of the Sixties Generation*. Ottowa, Ill.: Jameson Books, 1995.

Paul, John A., ed. *Civil Society: Theory, History, Comparison*. Cambridge, Mass.: Polity, 1995.

Portes, Alejandro. "Social Capital: Its Origins and Applications in Modern Sociology." *Annual Reviews in Sociology* 24 (1998): 1–24.

Pugah, Marleen C. *On the Border of Opportunity: Education, Community, and Language at the U.S.-Mexico Line*. Mahwah, N.J.: Lawrence Erlbaum, 1998.

Putman, Robert D. "Bowling Alone: America's Declining Social Capital." *Journal of Democracy* 6, no. 1 (January 1995): 65–78.

———. *Bowling Alone: The Collapse and Revival of American Community*. New York: Simon and Schuster, 2000.

———. *Making Democracy Work: Civic Traditions in Modern Italy*. Princeton: Princeton University Press, 1993.

Richmond, George H. *The Micro-Society School: A Real World in Miniature*. New York: Harper & Row, 1973.

Rogers, Mary Beth. *Cold Anger: A Story of Faith and Power Politics*. Denton: University of North Texas, 1990.

Romo, Harriett D., and Toni Falbo. *Latino High School Graduation: Defying the Odds*. Austin: University of Texas Press, 1996.

Roncha, Gregory G., and Robert H. Webking. *Politics and Public Education: Edgewood v. Kirby and the Reform of Public School Financing in Texas*. Minneapolis: West, 1992.

Rosenbaum, Robert J. *Mexicano Resistance in the Southwest: "The Sacred Right of Self-Preservation."* Austin: University of Texas Press, 1981.

Ruiz, Vicki L., and Susan Tiano, eds. *Women on the U.S.-Mexico Border: Responses to Change*. Boston: Allen and Unwin, 1987.

San Miguel Jr., Guadalupe. *"Let All of Them Take Heed": Mexican Americans and the Campaign for Educational Equality in Texas, 1910–1981*. Austin: University of Texas Press, 1987.

San Miguel Jr., Guadalupe, and Richard R. Valencia. "From the Treaty of Guadalupe Hidalgo to *Hopwood:* The Educational Plight and Struggle of Mexican Americans in the Southwest." *Harvard Educational Review* 68, no. 3 (1998): 353–412.

Sanders, Heywood T. "Communities Organized for Public Services and Neighborhood Revitalization in San Antonio." In *Public Policy and Community*, 36–68.

Sarason, Seymour. *The Predictable Failure of School Reform*. San Francisco: Jossey-Bass, 1990.

Sekul, Joseph D. "Communities Organized for Public Service: Citizen Power and Public Policy in San Antonio." In *The Politics of San Antonio: Community, Progress, and Power,* edited by David R. Johnson, John A. Booth, and Richard J. Harris, 175–90. Lincoln: University of Nebraska Press, 1983.

Shirley, Dennis. *Community Organizing for Urban School Reform.* Austin: University of Texas Press, 1997.

Skerry, Peter. *Mexican Americans: The Ambivalent Minority.* New York: Free Press, 1993.

Skocpol, Theda, and Richard C. Leone. *The Missing Middle: Working Families and the Future of American Social Policy.* New York: W. W. Norton, 2000.

Stanton-Salazar, Ricardo D. "A Social Capital Framework for Understanding the Socialization of Racial Minority Children and Youths." *Harvard Educational Review* 67, no. 1 (spring 1997): 1–40.

Steinberg, Lawrence. *Beyond the Classroom.* New York: Simon and Schuster, 1996.

Suárez-Orozco, Carola, and Marcelo M. Suárez-Orozco. *Transformations: Immigration, Family Life, and Achievement Motivation among Latino Adolescents.* Stanford: Stanford University Press, 1995.

Suárez-Orozco, Marcelo M., ed. *Crossings: Mexican Immigration in Interdisciplinary Perspectives.* Cambridge: Harvard University Press, 1998.

Suro, Roberto. *Strangers among Us: How Latino Immigration Is Transforming America.* New York: Knopf, 1998.

Tamez, Elsa, ed. *Through Her Eyes: Women's Theology from Latin America.* Maryknoll, N.Y.: Orbis, 1989.

Tharp, Roland G., and Ronald Gallimore. *Rousing Minds to Life: Teaching, Learning, and Schooling in the Social Context.* Cambridge: Cambridge University Press, 1998.

Toch, Thomas. *In the Name of Excellence.* New York: Oxford University Press, 1991.

Tocqueville, Alexis de. *Democracy in America.* 1838. Reprint, Garden City, N.Y.: Anchor, 1969.

———. *The Old Regime and the French Revolution.* 1856. Reprint, Garden City, N.Y.: Anchor, 1955.

Tovar, Consuelo. "Senator Learns We Mean Business." In *Organizing for Change: IAF, 50 Years,* edited by Cynthia Perry, 23. Franklin Square, N.Y.: Industrial Areas Foundation, 1990.

Trueba, Enrique. "The Education of Mexican Immigrant Children." In *Crossings: Mexican Immigration in Interdisciplinary Perspectives,* edited by Marcelo M. Suárez-Orozco. Cambridge: Harvard University Press, 1998.

Valencia, Richard R., ed. *Chicano School Failure and Success: Research and Policy Agendas for the 1990s*. Philadelphia: Falmer, 1991.

Valenzuela, Angela. *Subtractive Schooling: U.S.-Mexican Youth and the Politics of Caring*. Albany: State University of New York Press, 1999.

Vasquez, Olga A., Lucinda Pease-Alvarez, and Sheila M. Shannon. *Pushing Boundaries: Language and Culture in a Mexicano Community*. Cambridge: Cambridge University Press, 1994.

Vélez-Ibáñez, Carlos G. *Border Visions: Mexican Cultures of the Southwestern United States*. Tucson: University of Arizona Press, 1996.

Verhovek, Sam Howe. "Benefits of Free-Trade Pact Bypass Texas Border Towns." *New York Times*, 23 June 1998.

Viadero, Debra. "Testing System in Texas Yet to Get Final Grade." *Education Week*, 31 May 2000.

Vygotsky, L. S. *Mind in Society: The Development of Higher Psychological Processes*. Cambridge: Harvard University Press, 1978.

Weeks, John R., and Roberto Ham-Chande, eds. *Demographic Dynamics of the U.S.- Mexico Border*. El Paso: Texas Western Press, 1992.

Weil, Simone. *The Need for Roots: Prelude to a Declaration of Duties toward Mankind*. New York: Routledge, 1952.

Wendorf, Gregg. "Tired Yet of Local Politics?" *Advance News Journal*, 14 May 1997.

White, Julie A., and Gary Wehlage. "Community Collaboration: If It Is Such a Good Idea Why Is It So Hard to Do?" *Educational Evaluation and Policy Analysis* 17, no.1 (spring 1995): 23–28.

Wilson, Robert H., ed. *Public Policy and Community: Activism and Governance in Texas*. Austin: University of Texas Press, 1997.

Wilson, Robert H., and Peter Menzies. "The Colonias Water Bill: Communities Demanding Change." In *Public Policy and Community*, 229–74.

Wong, Pat. "The Indigent Healthcare Package." In *Public Policy and Community*, 95–118.

Zambrana, Ruth E., ed. *Work, Family, and Health: Latino Women in Transition*. Bronx, N.Y.: Hispanic Research Center, 1982.

Zamora, Emilio. *The World of the Mexican Worker in Texas*. College Station: Texas A&M University Press, 1993.

Zinn, Maxine Baca. "Mexican-American Women in the Social Sciences." *Signs: Journal of Women in Culture and Society* 8, no.2 (winter 1982): 259–72.

INDEX

Kozol, Jonathan, 100

League of United Latin American
    Citizens, 1, 2, 28
Levy, Frank, 99
Limón, José, xxi
Lopez, José, 66
Loury, Glenn, xv
Lucey, Robert, 3
LULAC, 1, 2, 28
Lytle, Susan, 91

Maheshwari, Connie, 63, 67–
    70, 74, 76, 80, 82, 86, 88–89,
    103–104
Martinez, Robert, 45, 49
MAYO (Mexican American Youth
    Organization), 2–3, 5
McAllen, Texas, 17–23, 46, 71–72
    Alliance Schools and, 66–67
    Barrios in, 63–64, 71–74, 78,
        86–87, 95
    Department of Parks and
        Recreation and, 69
McCluskey, Tim, 9
McNeil, Linda, 91
Meno, Lionel (Skip), 38
Mexican Americans, 1, 50, 52, 104
    Catholic church and, 88–90
    community organizing and,
        xii, 1, 5, 7
    educational reform and xi, xii
    immigration and, xi, 1, 7
    women, 89–90
Mexican American Unity Coun-
    cil, 4
Mexican American Youth Orga-
    nization, 2–3, 5
Milpas, Las, 14–16, 21, 24, 35–36,
    61, 63, 86, 100
Mindiz-Melton, Alejandro, 70
Mirandé, Alfredo, 89
Moll, Luis, 94

Montalvo, Leo, 17, 77
Montejano, David, 2
Murnane, Richard, 99

National Assessment of Educa-
    tional Progress, 85
Nayola, Oliver, 49, 54
North American Free Trade
    Agreement, xix

Padilla, Gil, 2
Palacios, Leo, 36
Palmer Elementary School, xx,
    xxii, 43, 83–84, 94
    academic achievement and, 84
    Alliance School network and,
        33–34
    community engagement and,
        27–28
    demographics of, 27
    dual-language program and,
        32–33, 41–42
    Ernie Cortés and, 29
    history of, 26–27
    home visits and, 30–32
    parental engagement and,
        24–42
    Salvador Flores and, 25–27, 29
    social capital and, 29
    TAAS and, 38–42, 105
    Valley Interfaith and, 29–30,
        33, 42
Paredes, Américo, xxi
Parental engagement, xvi, 34–37,
    41, 47–48, 86, 103–105
    academic achievement and, 39
Parental involvement, xvi, 34, 37,
    94, 104
Parent-Teacher Organization, 46
Parra, Javier, 8, 15–16
PASSO (Political Association of
    Spanish-Speaking Organiza-
    tions), 2

Pauken, Tom, 17–19, 22
Perot, H. Ross, 10, 21
Pharr, Texas, 24–25, 34, 36, 86–87
Pharr–San Juan–Alamo
   High School, 43–44, 52, 87
   Independent School District,
   34, 38–39, 51
Political Association of Spanish-
   Speaking Organizations, 2
Portes, Alejandro, xv, xvi
Project QUEST, 73
PSJA. *See* Pharr–San Juan–Alamo
Putnam, Robert, xv

Ramirez, René, 43–53
Raza Unida, 3, 5, 17
Reagan, Ronald, 18–19
Republican Party, 20
Research methodology, xxi–xxii
Richards, Ann, xxii, 9, 14–16
Rio Grande Valley, xviii–xxii
   Alliance Schools and, 83–84,
   91, 93
   Anglo-American settlement
   of, xvii–xix, 1
   Catholic church and, 12, 88
   community organizing and,
   4–6
   economic conditions in, xix, 5,
   7–9, 52, 72
   environmental conditions in,
   xix, 5, 9, 63
   history of, 1
   Mexican American women
   and, 13
   political conditions in, 1–4,
   8–9, 22
   population of, 7
   recent population growth in,
   xix
   social conditions in, xx, 1–2, 4,
   5, 65
   Valley Interfaith and, 83

Rivera, Robert, 64
Rosales, Mary Ann, 78
Ross, Fred, 5
Ruiz, Rosi, 52–53, 57, 62, 97

St. Joseph's the Worker Catholic
   Church, xxii, 23, 64–66, 73, 81,
   87–90, 94–95, 97, 101, 103
Salinas, Norberto, 17
Sam Houston Elementary School,
   xxi, xxii, 63–84, 86–91
   academic achievement and,
   84
   Alliance School Partnership
   and, 67, 80
   civic education and, 76–77
   curriculum development and,
   74–77
   Kids Action Assembly and, 71
   Los Encinos and, 71–74
   parents and, 68–69, 71–74,
   78–79
   social capital and, 87–88
   South Texas Community College and, 73
   TAAS and, 80–82, 105
   Valley Interfaith and, 64, 67–
   69, 72
Sanchez, Ermilia, 45
Sanchez, Maria, 66
Sarmiento, Susanna, 78, 91–92
Schumacher, Robert, 71–72, 87
Select Committee on Public Education, 10, 21
Social capital, xiv–xvii, 5–6, 46–
   47, 93, 100
   academic achievement and, xv,
   xvii
   bonding social capital, 5, 103
   bridging social capital, 46,
   89–90, 95, 97, 100–101, 103
   Catholic schools and, xv, xvi
   functionalism and, xviii